Bill Chastain

HarperCollins
LEADERSHIP
An Imprint of HarperCollins

THE
TARGET
STORY

How the Iconic
Big Box Store Hit the Bullseye and
Created an Addictive Retail Experience

Published by HarperCollins Leadership, an imprint of HarperCollins Focus LLC.

Published in association with Kevin Anderson & Associates: https://www.ka-writing.com/.

Book design by Aubrey Khan, Neuwirth & Associates.

ISBN 978-1-4002-1895-0 (eBook)
ISBN 978-1-4002-1894-3 (HC)

Library of Congress Control Number: 2020941536

20 21 22 23 LSC 10 9 8 7 6 5 4 3 2 1

CONTENTS

THE
TARGET
STORY

1902

George Draper Dayton forms Dayton Dry Goods Company, a department store that would become Target Corporation.

1946

The Dayton Company establishes the practice of giving 5 percent of pretax profits back to the community.

1962

Target's first grand opening takes place in Roseville, Minnesota, debuting the store's classic Bullseye logo.

1979

Target reaches $1 billion in annual sales.

1994

Target Stores unveils its brand promise: "Expect More. Pay Less."

1997

Target launches Take Charge of Education and donates up to 1 percent of Target REDcard purchases to eligible K-12 schools.

2005

Target exceeds $50 billion in annual sales.

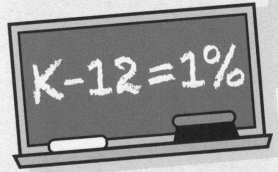

2019
Target celebrates the twentieth anniversary of its first designer partnership as a purveyor of chic, affordable design.

2017
The "focus on Owned Brands" is personified with the introduction of a dozen new brands within eighteen months.

 2015
CVS Health acquires Target's pharmacy and clinic businesses, operating them within Target stores.

2014
Target accelerates its $100 million plan to move its REDcard portfolio to chip-and-PIN-enabled technology.

2010
Target announces its goal to contribute $1 billion toward education by the end of 2015.

2009
The AIA presents a Presidential Citation to Target recognizing its corporate commitment to design.

2007
Target celebrates the milestone of giving more than $3 million per week to local communities.

"If we're doing
the right things for
our communities, and
making communities
stronger, our business
will also benefit."

—**BRIAN CORNELL,** Target CEO

CHAPTER ONE

FOUNDING STORY

Target's brand promise is simple, yet complex: "Expect more. Pay less."

Fulfilling that idealistic promise requires expertise in areas like supply chain, inventory control, replenishment, merchandising, marketing, customer service, advertising, and innovation to name a few. Putting all those pieces together, working as one, has enabled the retail giant to "help all families discover the joy of everyday life."[1] Satisfying "guests" is the secret sauce that has fueled Target's immense success.

Today, Target has over 350,000 employees and operates stores in all fifty states and in the District of Columbia. Approximately 75 percent of the US population lives within ten miles of a Target store, giving them easy accessibility. The company is a talent-based organization that is heavily immersed in its culture and core values. Those values and the culture have evolved to reflect a more modern-day retail organization, yet the purpose of helping all families discover joy is grounded in the chain's foundation.

" Today, Target has over 350,000 employees and operates stores in all fifty states and in the District of Columbia. Approximately 75 percent of the US population lives within ten miles of a Target store, giving them easy accessibility.

"I think that there are some principles that have been long lasting in the company," said Brian Cornell, Target CEO and chairman. "The focus on giving back. . . . And this general belief that if we're doing the right things for our communities, and making communities stronger, our business will also benefit. But I think that goes all the way back to the founding family."[2]

How It All Began

George Draper Dayton was born on March 6, 1857, in Clifton Springs, New York, in the western part of the state.

The Daytons' family lineage could be traced back to Ralph Dayton, a shoemaker who arrived to the New World in the 1600s from County Kent, England. Ralph eventually settled in East Hampton, New York, where he served as the town's constable as well as an interpreter to the Native Americans. Another relative, Jonathan Dayton, earned recognition as a New Jersey politician and for being the youngest to sign the United States Constitution; Dayton, Ohio, was named after him.

George's parents, David and Caroline Dayton, were a religious couple. David was a successful doctor and surgeon as well as a devout Presbyterian; his wife was a Methodist. Their actions set an altruistic example for George, who gravitated to the church. After passing the entrance exam for Hobart College in 1873, he hoped to enroll and study to become a minister. But his plans changed when the Panic of 1873 thrust the country into a depression.

George had worked at a nursery since the age of eleven, where he made 37½ cents a day. He continued to work at the nursery the summer after finishing high school in Clifton, New York. That fall of 1873, his father took note of how many businesses were already experiencing financial difficulty. George McMillan ran one of the stressed businesses and asked Dr. Dayton for financial help. That led Dr. Dayton to offer an apprenticeship for his son's services.[3] McMillan, who had his hands in a number of businesses, including lumber and coal interests, paid George a salary of $800 per year with a 3 percent commission. George took the job, operating on the belief that he would build a nest egg for himself before following through with his college plans. Though he was only sixteen, George had a work ethic that caught McMillan off guard. He had not fathomed that George would earn any commission. But George's ambition led him to solicit sales in the evenings.[4] George wrote the following about the experience: "I had drawn very little of the salary, so around fifteen hundred dollars were due and Mr. McMillan could not pay. He suggested I buy the coal and lumberyard."[5]

George borrowed money from his father and became owner of the business at seventeen. While his work ethic helped him thrive in his business, the hours he kept eventually took their toll. After trying to work consecutive twenty-four-hour shifts, he got sick, prompting Dr. Dayton to sell his son's business and help him regain his health. When George recovered, he returned to the workplace with perspective. John Mackay, who owned a lumberyard and had a banking business, hired Dayton.

> **Though he was only sixteen, George had a work ethic that caught McMillan off guard. He had not fathomed that George would earn any commission. But George's ambition led him to solicit sales in the evenings, and by the end of the year, he had earned approximately $1,500. McMillan could not pay, so he suggested that George buy the coal and lumberyard.**

Through investments and the sale of his business, George managed to save $5,000 by age twenty-one, paving the way for him to marry his longtime sweetheart, Emma Chadwick, on December 17, 1878, in Montour Falls, New York.

George Goes to Minneapolis

Emma's parents were both heavily invested in education. Her father, Edmund C. Chadwick, a professor, had even been a classmate and personal friend of Ralph Waldo Emerson. Emma quite naturally was drawn to her profession as a teacher.[6]

Having experienced the struggles created by a lack of money, George and Emma agreed to set aside $5 every week, putting into place a shared habit of saving.

Among George's duties while working for Mackay were to be in charge of his office and banking business. Typical of George, he had wowed Mackay with his business acumen, as well as New York investors, who were so impressed by George's business mind, judgment, and integrity that they enlisted him to help with their mortgage holdings in the Midwest. They sent George to Worthington, Minnesota, to gain insight into why the investments they'd made through the local bank, the Bank of Worthington, had gone south. George followed instructions, then reported back to the New York investors that Minnesota farmers had suffered a six-year run of bad luck that included a grasshopper scourge and bad weather. The effects of those circumstances had proved devastating, prompting many to leave behind their farms and their debts. George suggested that the investors ought to put somebody in place locally to look after their investments. They agreed and urged George to become that guy. Backed by investors, he bought the Bank of Worthington and moved to Worthington to take charge of the bank in April of 1883.[7]

George sorted out the bank's bad mortgages and debts then resold the land, even convincing the New York investors to put more money into Worthington. That exercise led to his forming the Minnesota Loan & Investment Co. of Worthington, which concentrated on buying and selling farm property and lending money to farmers.

By the 1890s, George and his cohorts at Minnesota Loan & Investment expanded their interests to include city properties. George checked out the prospects for several cities, including Salt Lake City, St. Paul, Omaha, St. Louis, Kansas City, and Minneapolis.[8] Minneapolis served as a railroad hub and boasted of healthy lumber and flour mill industries on the Mississippi River, which influenced George's decision. He never looked back, immersing himself in what would become a lifelong love affair with Minneapolis and its community.

Executing his due diligence as he began his search for prime real estate, George would count people on downtown street corners. "As I was not known by many in the city, I felt free to stand on corners and count the people pass," Dayton said.[9]

Most figured the logical, and best, prospects for downtown real estate would be in close proximity to the flour mills and the Mississippi River. George's research told him otherwise, directing him to concentrate his purchases along Nicollet Avenue, between Fourth and Tenth Streets, or "uptown" as opposed to "downtown."[10] Dayton's strategy proved wise, increasing his wealth while expanding his interests in the evolving Midwestern city.

The Fire

Fire brought a constant threat to Minneapolis in the late nineteenth century. The area had sustained droughts in 1893 and 1894, which left the city parched and ripe to go up in flames with the slightest spark. On August 13, 1893, the most devastating fire in the city's history occurred, igniting approximately twenty-three city blocks.

By 1895, however, conditions had changed, due in large part to the end of the drought. The total number of alarms sounded dropped 30 percent, and the losses due to fire were reduced by 45 percent.[11] Still, two memorable fires dotted the Minneapolis landscape that year.

A June 27 fire at MacDonald Brothers' crockery warehouse left five firefighters dead, the worst loss of life in the Minneapolis Fire Department's history. Less than three months later, the Westminster Presbyterian Church caught fire in the early morning of September 6, 1895. A general alarm rang out at around 2:30 a.m., sending firefighters to the church's location at the corner of Nicollet Avenue and Seventh Street. The fire had ignited in the roof over the main part of the large church. Getting water to the flames proved to be a logistical nightmare. By the time firefighters had extinguished the fire, the church had been destroyed.[12]

Bystanders from the surrounding neighborhoods had been awakened by the bells and whistles. They watched the fire department's efforts and were astounded when the roof gave way. Critiques of the department followed. Surely, if they had located the fire hoses in a more strategic fashion, the church would not have met its fate.[13]

The fire left the church in a pickle. Rebuilding wasn't in the cards because its insurance failed to cover the cost of the damage. And the prospects for selling were dismal since real estate had tumbled due to a recession.[14] Several Minneapolis business leaders looked to George Dayton to help rectify the church's problem. He came through, buying the distressed property early in 1896 for $165,000.[15]

Allen Hill, the secretary of the Westminster board of trustees, expressed gratitude following the transaction. "I do not know what Mr. Dayton's intentions are with regard to the property, but I do know that we feel relieved that the matter has finally settled. The price we consider but a fair one, and now the church feels at liberty to take immediate steps toward the purchase of a location and the erection of a new church."[16]

Dayton's plans remained unclear, but he continued to purchase property in the proximity of the Westminster lot until he
possessed full frontage along Nicollet Avenue between Seventh
and Eighth Streets.[17] The Westminster property remained an
eyesore, even after Dayton's purchase, prompting Minneapolis
building inspector John A. Gilman to notify Dayton that the
remaining walls were unsafe and needed to be removed.[18]

Dayton made a deal to sell the property to a group of Chicago investors, who had grandiose plans for the Westminster
church site. After a prolonged negotiation, the Chicago investors agreed to buy it for $2,000 per front foot on the 215 feet
on Nicollet Avenue, where they planned to build a fireproof,
ten-story, European-style hotel. Several details of the agreement
needed to be worked out before the deal was finalized, but the
Chicago group had enough confidence about the project going forward that they hired an architect to rush plans for the
$500,000 hotel. However, when one of the investors visited Min-
neapolis, he learned that the proposed hotel would be located
in a dry zone, meaning the hotel's bar would not be able to
serve alcohol. That detail turned into a deal-breaker. The investor wired his partners to tell them what he told Dayton, that the
deal was "dead as a door nail."[19]

Finally, Dayton decided to build a six-story building on the
Westminster site. The building covered 215 feet on Nicollet
Avenue and 140 feet on Seventh Street and would be composed
of brick, iron, plate glass, and the "latest patterns" in pressed
brick and terra cotta.[20]

Construction began in 1901 and was completed in 1902.
Dayton's solution for having a tenant came when he convinced
the R.S. Goodfellow Company, Minneapolis's fourth-largest department store, to move into the building. Dayton bought a
share of retiring owner Reuben Simon Goodfellow's interest

in the store. Believing that Minneapolis's citizens wanted to patronize businesses that were operated by locals, Dayton persuaded several residents to become part of the venture's ownership.[21] J.B. Mosher, a local businessman with a wealth of retail experience, and George London, a longtime Goodfellow's employee, bought the other shares of Goodfellow's interest. Dayton wanted to remain in the background as a silent partner and harbored no aspirations of becoming a merchant.[22]

Along with the change in ownership came a new name, Goodfellow Dry Goods Co. A soft opening took place on June 2, 1902. The formal opening of the store followed twenty-two days later. The new store—referred to as the "Daylight" store—offered virtually anything a shopper might want, from high fashion to practical items. According to the *Minneapolis Journal*'s account of the store's formal opening, "There is plenty of 'elbow' and breathing room, and the store is immaculate from its splendid basement to its sixth floor."[23]

> **Along with the change in ownership came a new name, Goodfellow Dry Goods Co. The new store—referred to as the "Daylight" store—offered virtually anything a shopper might want, from high fashion to practical items.**

A New Venture

Corresponding with the store's opening, Dayton moved his family from Worthington to Minneapolis. He and his wife now had four children: Draper, Caroline, Nelson, and Josephine. On July 14, 1902, he sold his house in Worthington, had all of his family's belongings loaded onto a railroad car, and headed to Minneapolis to begin a new adventure in the city.

Despite the grandiose nature of the formal opening, many local businessmen believed that Dayton had missed the mark with his enterprise and that he would lose his shirt. Others had passed on buying the Westminster property due to its location in the uptown area, away from the more popular loop district. But Dayton proved the naysayers wrong when Goodfellow Dry Goods Company doubled its sales in its first year. He then bought out one of his partners, who had shown himself to be shady in his financial dealings; shortly thereafter, he bought out the other partner.

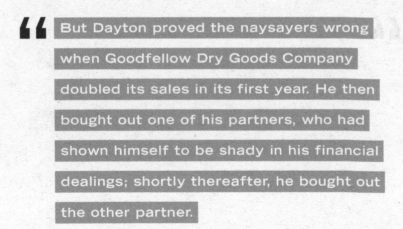

> But Dayton proved the naysayers wrong when Goodfellow Dry Goods Company doubled its sales in its first year. He then bought out one of his partners, who had shown himself to be shady in his financial dealings; shortly thereafter, he bought out the other partner.

Dayton pressed hard to turn increased sales into profitability, but never strayed from the virtuous path he traveled, which included providing to customers quality, service, and honesty. Finally, in 1906, the store turned the corner, realizing a profit for the first time.[24]

Dayton committed to offering customers a vast variety of options from tools to high-fashion clothes.[25] Dayton even went as far as to send an employee, Theodore Mayer, to Deauville, France, to study French styles in one of the most fashionable cities in the world. Upon his return, purchases from the trip became available in-store, and reproductions of the most beautiful wraps, gowns, and other fashions Mayer saw were made and sold to customers.[26]

Dayton's made sure its shelves were always fully stocked with merchandise, and the store would go to great lengths to ensure that nothing interfered with fulfilling this goal. In 1920, the railroad executed a freight embargo, which interfered with Dayton's ability to receive shipments. Demonstrating just how far the store would go to prevent shortages, Dayton's hired two airplanes to send eight hundred pounds of freight from New York to Minneapolis. It was the longest cargo-carrying flight ever made for commercial purposes.[27]

Dayton converted the basement floor to an area where customers could shop for items at lower prices. The assortment of less expensive merchandise included apparel for men, women, and children. Accessories, underwear, yard supplies, draperies—everything and anything. Customers who shopped in the basement weren't second-class citizens, either. They could eat lunch there and even get their shoes shined.[28] Dayton's also boasted what was described as a "generous" return policy.[29]

The prospect of entertaining the customers brought all kinds of innovative ideas. For example, "Russian tea in true Russian style" was held on the third floor during fashion week, and Dayton's offered a five-week course in dressmaking, which three hundred Minneapolis women participated in, and which climaxed with a style show.[30] But the "Little Mothers and Dolls Tea d'enfant" might have been the bravest. Three thousand girls ages three to twelve—without their mothers—were entertained during a two-hour event in which they drank "tiny cups of chocolate" and ate animal crackers without making so much as a peep.[31]

> "Russian tea in true Russian style" was held on the third floor during fashion week, and Dayton's offered a five-week course in dressmaking, which three hundred Minneapolis women participated in, and which climaxed with a style show. But the "Little Mothers and Dolls Tea d'enfant" might have been the bravest. Three thousand girls ages three to twelve—without their mothers—were entertained during a two-hour event in which they drank "tiny cups of chocolate" and ate animal crackers without making so much as a peep.

Dayton's held its first "Jubilee Bargain Sale" on October 12, 1922, an occasion that saw the store sell double of what it had on the largest days it had previously experienced. The following day, the store placed an ad in the *Minneapolis Morning Tribune* thanking its customers and adding: "We appreciate the confidence of the people of Minneapolis in our advertising and our merchandise—it imposes on us a greater responsibility for the future. We will strive always to merit that confidence."[32]

Company Culture and Charity

Dayton ran the store like a family business, and his beliefs spilled over into his business principles, which followed a strict Presbyterian ethos: Dayton's wasn't open for business on Sundays, the store did not sell alcohol, it did not allow business travel or advertise on the Sabbath, and it would not advertise in a newspaper with liquor ads.[33]

All the while, Dayton supported the community with his generosity and civic-minded efforts, which infused into the company's culture. By 1920, his store employed well over one thousand locals and held company-wide picnics on Lake Minnetonka in nearby Spring Park for over 1,700 Dayton employees and their guests.[34] At Christmas, Dayton's awarded annual bonuses equivalent to 2 percent of the sales.[35]

Later in Dayton's life, he spoke at Macalester College, a Presbyterian school in St. Paul, and delivered the following message, which offers insight into his philanthropic mind: "It sounds somewhat complex but really it is very simple. Business integrity can be defined to be: Doing things as you agreed to do them. Doing things when you agreed to do them. Doing the things that you ought to do."[36]

Dayton's religious upbringing instilled habits such as regular church attendance, tithing, and reading the Bible. Even before wealth found him, Dayton regularly tithed. Later in his life, he would remind church ministers about their responsibility to exalt the virtues of tithing from the pulpit. By the time George had reached the age of thirty, he gave 40 percent of his income to his church. But his charity didn't stop there. Dayton regularly matched donations to charities as a means of incentivizing others to give.

In 1918, he established the Dayton Foundation, which he created with the basic aim of helping anybody in need. Though he directed much of his giving—both personally and through the foundation—toward religious matters, such as ministers, missionaries, and Macalester College, he also supported nonreligious entities in need.

Dayton saw fit to make sure the company donated to charitable causes too.[37]

Because the company had not gone public, this was not an issue. The Minneapolis community viewed Dayton as a giver—someone who freely offered his money and time where matters of charity, public welfare, and religion were concerned. In addition to the Presbyterian Church, he was involved in the Minneapolis YWCA and the YMCA, the Union City Mission, and he also served as president of the board of trustees of Macalester, where he played a large role in the institution's development. Yet he considered using a majority of his personal fortune to establish the Dayton Foundation to be the most important achievement of his life.[38]

After George Dayton's death on February 18, 1938, the *Minneapolis Morning Tribune* wrote the following morning: "In the more than 50 years that Minnesota knew him as a citizen, it had countless occasions manifested itself, not in idle words or ostentation, but in good deeds humbly done."[39]

> After George Dayton's death on February 18, 1938, the *Minneapolis Morning Tribune* wrote the following morning: "In the more than 50 years that Minnesota knew him as a citizen, it had countless occasions manifested itself, not in idle words or ostentation, but in good deeds humbly done."

"We had a wonderful bunch of farmers to work with and you worked right alongside them. You couldn't take advantage of your position."

—BRUCE DAYTON
on the Dayton boys' upbringing

CHAPTER TWO

LIFE AFTER GEORGE DAYTON

Draper Dayton—George and Emma's oldest son—graduated from Princeton cum laude in 1902 and returned to Minneapolis to work in the department store at Nicollet and Seventh, which George Dayton had taken over only a few months before. Draper was born in Geneva, New York, prior to his parents moving to Worthington. He attended the Worthington schools before heading to Princeton, where his good nature earned him the nickname "Genial."[1]

Draper wanted to start at the bottom rung of the department store so he could learn the business, which he did. Through that beginning, Draper became one of Minneapolis's most successful businessmen, helping Dayton's become one of the largest and most contemporary department stores in the Midwest. He did so while embracing his father's ideals. The company's employees loved Draper, who always took interest in their well-being.[2]

Draper got promoted to general manager in 1906 at the age of twenty-six. Obviously, he had entered the company as the owner's son, but entering the business in the fashion that he did established him as his own man. Draper had a knack for merchandising and finance,[3] and believed the store should sell only quality merchandise at an honest value.[4]

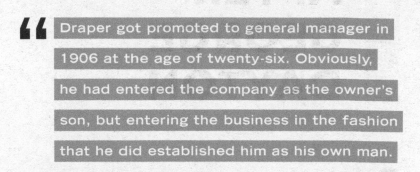

> *"* Draper got promoted to general manager in 1906 at the age of twenty-six. Obviously, he had entered the company as the owner's son, but entering the business in the fashion that he did established him as his own man.

Nelson Dayton—George and Emma's youngest son—attended Worthington schools like his brother, before attending Macalester College and the University of Minnesota. After graduating in 1906, he operated a farm for four years before his father and brother convinced him to join them at the company, where he first worked as a salesman in the blanket department. In 1911, each of the brothers bought a share in the company.[5]

A Management Shift

Draper died unexpectedly of heart disease in 1923 at age forty-three. Devastated by his son's death, George Dayton wanted to sell the store. But Nelson convinced him to stay the course. Nelson, who by now had worked his way up to a position in the general superintendent's office, became the store's general manager, which opened the door for his brilliance to surface. He formed an executive staff and brought in personnel that would help the company reach new heights.

Nelson became the Dayton Company's president upon his father's death in 1938, and the company continued to thrive under his leadership. Dayton's plant and facilities were expanded. Four stories were added to the corner of the store at Eighth Street and Nicollet Avenue in 1939. Six stories were added to the store's garage in 1946, the same year the Dayton's building grew to twelve stories. The company acquired the National Tea Company's warehouse, and constructed another that took up an entire city block.[6]

Nelson maintained the established Dayton way of doing things, which meant keeping a low profile while lending major assistance to philanthropic and civic efforts. In 1946, he made certain that the Dayton Company's established giving would continue after him by formalizing the company's policy of giving away 5 percent of pretax profits, the most federal law allowed at that time. Among United States companies, only S&H Green Stamps had a comparable giving policy at the time.[7] Nelson also established retirement packages and comprehensive insurance policies for his employees, who were always at the forefront of his mind.

Throughout, Nelson's interest in agriculture never waned. Remarkably, he displayed as much excellence in that field as he did as a businessman and merchant. On his Boulder Bridge Farm near Lake Minnetonka, he built the "Boulder Bridge" herd, an elite, prize-winning herd of Guernsey cattle that captured national titles and earned recognition as one of the country's top Guernsey herds.

Nelson had five sons, who all joined the business: Donald, Bruce, Wallace, Kenneth, and Douglas.[8] The importance of hard work and establishing a strong work ethic had been a part of their father's heritage. No doubt, Nelson felt the parental responsibility to do whatever necessary to ensure that his sons did not grow up with silver spoons in their mouths, despite the family's obvious prosperity. The boys spent their summers living and working at the Boulder Bridge Farm.

> " Nelson maintained the established Dayton way of doing things, which meant keeping a low profile while lending major assistance to philanthropic and civic efforts. In 1946, he made certain that the Dayton Company's established giving would continue after him by formalizing the company's policy of giving away 5 percent of pretax profits, the most federal law allowed at that time. Among United States companies, only S&H Green Stamps had a comparable giving policy at the time.

"We worked in the mornings for 10 cents an hour, down in the barns, and played in the afternoon," Bruce said. "I was a driver's helper on the farm truck, mostly what we hauled was manure. Load by hand, unload by hand. We had a wonderful bunch of farmers to work with and you worked right alongside them. You couldn't take advantage of your position."[9]

All of the boys also went to work at Dayton's, each performing low-level jobs initially. Donald, the eldest, had polio as a child, but overcame the disease and went on to compete for Yale University's swim team while majoring in government. However, the effects of having polio prevented him from being able to enlist for military service during the war, making him the only Dayton brother who didn't serve. Following their military service, each of the boys continued to work at the store.

Nelson Dayton died in 1950. When he'd taken charge of the operation, the Dayton company was a $14 million enterprise with approximately 1,500 employees. At the time of his death, the company had $50 million in annual sales with over four thousand employees.[10]

"Perhaps because we were a family-run business, we worked doubly hard to become highly professional ourselves and to instill professional management."

—KEN DAYTON

CHAPTER THREE

THE THIRD GENERATION

E ach of Nelson Dayton's sons received 20 percent of the business upon their father's death. Donald Dayton became president. Along with his four brothers, he led the company during the postwar era. Donald began at Dayton's in 1937, working as a stock boy and clerk before holding positions as a buyer, divisional merchandising manager, general superintendent, assistant general manager, and general manager. The board elected him president and CEO in 1960 and he became chairman of the board in 1965.[1] Bruce became chief financial officer; Wally, head of operations; Ken, general merchandising manager of apparel; and Doug, a merchandiser.

Dayton's held a regal place in the Minneapolis community, operating a quality store while being an outstanding corporate citizen. The company felt like family. According to a 1950 article in *Greater Minnesota Magazine,* Dayton's brought the feeling of being "all things to all people." The article also identified the company's philosophy as follows:

- To keep growing in size and prestige
- To sell dependable merchandise at a reasonable profit
- To serve the community in the broadest sense[2]

> **" The company felt like family. According to a 1950 article in *Greater Minnesota Magazine*, Dayton's brought the feeling of being "all things to all people."**

The Best Display of Playing Cards in Minneapolis

While the company's direction looked clear-cut in the article, that direction wasn't as concrete to the brothers. They had worked hard to maintain status quo following their father's death, but they had no solid vision for the future. In Bruce Dayton's book, *The Birth of Target*, the second eldest brother recalled an anecdote from that period, when he and his siblings were finding themselves and searching for a new identity. After Nelson's death, Oscar and Richard Webber—the owners of J. L. Hudson's Department Store in Detroit—as well as family friends, paid Dayton's a visit. Moving through the stationary department on the main floor, they pointed out a nondescript display of playing cards. They asked if the display could be considered the best display of playing cards in Minneapolis, adding, "Does every woman think of Dayton's first whenever she needs some playing cards? For the store to remain dominant, it must make every category in every department of the store dominant."[3]

The brothers began meeting for Saturday lunch at the Radisson Hotel next to the store to develop a strategy for the company's future. Businessmen worked six days a week in the early 1950s, and each of the brothers would do a walkthrough of the store every Saturday morning—afterward they would hold their informal lunch meeting. Collectively, they set the goal of sorting through their situation and deciding on a definitive direction in which the store should proceed.

"We had a hell of a responsibility just to keep things going," Donald said.[4] The brothers were close and got along extremely well. That translated into an ability to find collaborative solutions. If their discussions did not bring them to an agreement, they would take a quick vote on the matter at hand and require a three-out-of-five majority to make their decision.[5]

America had begun the transition into a new era. The birth of the baby boomers spoke to a rapidly growing population; meanwhile, the passage of the Servicemen's Readjustment Act of 1944—or the G.I. Bill—made low-interest mortgages and money for college, trade schools, and businesses readily available to returning veterans. This triggered a housing boom, and residential construction rose from 114,000 new homes in 1944 to 1.7 million in 1950.[6] Suburbs were created to facilitate the construction of these new homes—and baby boomer prosperity also brought an increased demand for consumer products.

Dayton's sat at a crossroads. The brothers understood that times were changing. They didn't want to get caught clinging to the past. The flagship store was in need of renovations, and a handful of the store's leading managers had retired in the years prior to Nelson's death. Discovering what Dayton's lacked became a focus of the brothers' weekly lunch.

They made an evaluation of where Dayton's stood in comparison to other retailers, identifying other major players in the arena. How did they all stack up in regards to balance sheets, sales, and profits? The brothers came up with the following:

1. The premier, top level of retailers included national companies such as Sears, Roebuck & Company, J. C. Penney Company, and Federated Department Stores, Inc., a holding company for department stores such as Abraham & Straus, Filene's, and Bloomingdale's.
2. The middle tier included chains such as May Department Stores Company, Allied Stores Corporation, and Associated Dry Goods.
3. The lower tier included smaller retailers such as single-store, family-owned retailers, like Dayton's.[7]

The brothers agreed that maintaining the status quo at Dayton's would have been the easy way out. They wanted more.

Seeking larger profits in an explosive economy would be the responsible path. That meant growth. But how? They questioned whether they had the expertise to guide Dayton's into a growth mode; however, they did not allow that collective insecurity to handicap them.

Improving their store became the first step: make Dayton's even more dominant by enhancing each department, establishing solid advertising, and staging special events.

Building a management team was critical. The brothers wanted to put together a management team that could outperform them, and they also wanted to expand the store's merchandising team. That led to a three-part development plan, which necessitated innovation.[8]

A New Addition

In 1954, they opened their second department store, a six-and-one-half-story modern version of their flagship location, in close proximity to the Mayo Clinic in Rochester, Minnesota.

The Rochester store was a contemporary, windowless space with all the bells and whistles, including a temperature-controlled interior and heated sidewalks that prevented snow from blocking potential shoppers. The store did well immediately, thanks to these modern innovations, along with some good, old-fashioned luck. IBM had located a branch division in Rochester in 1953, boosting the local economy, along with the newly built Dayton's.

" In 1954, they opened their second department store, a six-and-one-half-story modern version of their flagship location, in close proximity to the Mayo Clinic in Rochester, Minnesota. The Rochester store was a contemporary, windowless space with all the bells and whistles, including a temperature-controlled interior and heated sidewalks that prevented snow from blocking potential shoppers. The store did well immediately, thanks to these modern innovations, along with some good, old-fashioned luck.

The Rochester opening was accompanied by a change in Dayton's advertising policy. Now Dayton's only ran advertisements Monday through Friday. Hoping to lure regional customers from Minnesota's far-reaching areas, as well as North and South Dakota and Wisconsin, Dayton's began to run ads in the *Minneapolis Sunday Tribune*, whose readership had a geographical reach.

In November of 1954, the brothers purchased Fantle's Department Store in Sioux Falls, South Dakota. Giving the company a foothold toward the west had been the thinking behind this strategic purchase. Dayton's continued to operate the 54,000-square-foot store under the Fantle's name. The store, however, did not meet projections. In March of 1967, Dayton's sold Dayton's Sioux Falls—the wholly owned subsidiary that operated Fantle's. Dayton's learned a lesson and sold, deciding that future long-range plans would "concentrate its business in major metropolitan markets."[9]

Shopping for All Seasons

Part three of the Dayton brothers' plan was triggered in part by a study Donald Dayton commissioned that confirmed what most knew: two-thirds of the year brought suboptimal shopping days in the Minneapolis area due to the climate. The brothers therefore enlisted Victor Gruen, an iconic Viennese architect, to bring to life a place where weather would not hinder the shopping experience. Not only did Gruen carry a highly visible public profile, but he also brought along a compelling story.

Educated at the Vienna Academy of Fine Arts, where he studied architecture, Gruen and his wife fled his homeland in

1938, assisted by a friend dressed as a Nazi storm trooper. The journey placed Gruen in New York City with just eight dollars in his pocket.[10]

> Two-thirds of the year brought sub-optimal shopping days in the Minneapolis area due to the climate. The brothers therefore enlisted Victor Gruen, an iconic Viennese architect, to bring to life a place where weather would not hinder the shopping experience.

Gruen could not speak English, but he did have a degree in architecture. Eventually, he ran into a friend from Vienna, who hired him to design a boutique on Fifth Avenue. The completed product's design featured a unique mini-arcade in the entranceway that served as a "customer trap." The boutique's success firmly established him, and Gruen became well sought after for projects around the country. In the early 1950s, he designed Northland, J.L. Hudson's outdoor shopping center located in a Detroit suburb.[11] Built in 1954, the two-million-square-foot complex contained a supermarket, a bank, auditoriums, and a post office, affording consumers a place where they could take care of their many needs without having to drive downtown.

With Gruen in the fold, the Dayton brothers swung for the fences, acquiring five hundred acres for their ambitious project. "It was a major step," Don Dayton said. "The land was in the sticks but not far from where Dayton's best customers lived. . . . There were people out there, and somebody was going to supply them with merchandise and services. We could lose the business to ourselves by building a branch store, or we could lose it to our competition. We *had* to go there."[12]

Gruen's and Donald Dayton's plan to create Southdale, a unique shopping venue in Endina, Minnesota, was unveiled in 1952. To deal with the weather, Gruen designed a shopping venue with many stores that were all located inside—complete with heat in the winter and air-conditioning in the summer. Escalators connected the two-floor structure, which also boasted two-tiered parking. A "town center" feel could be found in the courtyard area—one of the country's largest indoor public spaces—which featured hanging plants, works of art, a café, trees, a fishpond, and a cage filled with exotic birds.[13]

Gruen believed shopping centers should display artwork because merchants were art patrons. Accordingly, he believed Southdale could "be to our time what the church and nobility were to the Middle Ages."[14]

Donald Dayton said of the United States' first indoor-shopping mall, "We plan to make our own weather at Southdale. Every day will be fair and mild."[15] Southdale had no exterior windows, which proved to be a stroke of retail genius. The unimpeded sight lines, trees, and lighting kept consumers from discerning the amount of time they had actually spent shopping.[16]

Southdale Center came at a cost of $20 million, and boasted seventy-two stores on eighty thousand square feet.[17]

Dayton's and Donaldson's became the mall's two anchor tenants, which surprised many since Donaldson's had long been Dayton's chief retail rival; the stores stared at each other across Nicollet Avenue at Seventh Street in downtown

Minneapolis.[18] Why had Dayton's reached out to Donaldson's to open a store inside their mall? Bruce Dayton's explanation revealed the brothers' unique business strategy. "Our studies indicated clearly that a successful shopping center must include a strong community of competing business neighbors each as accessible as the nucleus. This increases the drawing power greatly and allows comparative shopping."[19]

Southdale had no exterior windows, which proved to be a stroke of retail genius. The unimpeded sight lines, trees, and lighting kept consumers from discerning the amount of time they had actually spent shopping. Southdale Center came at a cost of $20 million, and boasted seventy-two stores on eighty thousand square feet.

Southdale Center's opening gala took place on October 8, 1956, and 75,000 people attended, followed by another 188,000 visitors the following weekend.[20] Not only had Southdale Center delivered an innovative venue for retail shopping—casting a template for shopping experiences across the country—it also introduced a creative method for vendors supplying stores. Rather than having to use inside or outside entrances to make their deliveries, vendors were able to do so via a thirty-foot-wide underground tunnel with loading docks that served every store.[21]

In the aftermath of Southdale's immediate success, the Dayton brothers decided their plans for growth would entail using expansion and acquisitions to develop business, build shopping centers throughout the Twin Cities area, and try out specialty stores in Southdale, where they could open and close businesses almost at will since they owned the property. In conjunction with expanding the company's reach, the Dayton brothers continued to buy land and opened Dayton Development Company to manage its real estate properties.

Grooming the Future

The Dayton brothers understood the importance of quality management. Talented merchandising professionals could be found within the company; however, professional managers educated in the science of business management were rare. Even the Dayton brothers lacked formal educations in this area. They had assumed management roles through ownership and serving apprenticeships while growing up in the company underneath their father's leadership.[22]

One solution to the lack of management expertise was to reach outside the company and hire qualified professionals. Among the notable hires from the outside were:

Stuart W. Wells, who had been an investment banker, a salesman for R.H. Macy in New York, and a designer for Bergdorf Goodman of New York, before Dayton's hired him from Young-Quinlan in Minneapolis.[23] He would rise to president of the department store division of the Dayton Corp.[24]

Hadlai A. Hull, who had a distinguished military career before Dayton's hired him from Minnesota & Ontario Paper

Co.,[25] and advanced to the Dayton Company's chief financial officer. After his retirement from Dayton's, he accepted a position as Assistant Secretary of the Army.[26]

John A. Curry was hired from General Mills and advanced to vice president and corporate controller of Dayton Corp.[27]

Bruce had already taken several steps to further his own management skills, and each of the remaining Dayton brothers followed his lead by participating in an executive course taught at Cornell University that addressed annual reviews, setting objectives and goals, creating job descriptions, and implementing various other management techniques. These exercises brought an increased awareness of the company's need to groom its own professional management.[28] The Daytons developed guidelines for doing so, which called for the following:

- Developing job descriptions for department and work-center management positions on up
- Setting annual goals and objectives for the corporation and each division, company, department, and work center (such as a stock room or mail center)
- Quarterly reviews of performance in reference to the goals and objectives at the appropriate level
- Annual performance reviews based on job descriptions, the results of the previous year's review, and current goals and objectives
- Rewards based on obtaining results related to the goals and objectives set for the preceding year[29]

"We were nuts on professionalism," wrote Ken Dayton in July 2001. "Perhaps because we were a family-run business . . .

we worked doubly hard to become highly professional ourselves and to instill professional management throughout the
business."[30]

Moving forward, every executive in the company would be
evaluated on a regular basis, and so would their job descriptions. Employees were incentivized and rewarded at every level.
This led to harmony and kept everybody in the same boat and
rowing in the same direction.

Dayton's, along with three local heavyweights—Honeywell,
Northwest Bancorporation, and General Mills—eventually
banded together to create a school to collectively train their
executives and managers.[31] The "Four Company Program"
was unique—no other city in America offered anything
comparable—and proved cost-efficient. Dayton's had developed a highly effective means for refining leadership: the
brothers' push toward becoming a more professional, corporate entity—rather than simply maintaining the status quo as a
family operation—had paid off in a big way.

" Employees were incentivized and rewarded at every level. This led to harmony and kept everybody in the same boat and rowing in the same direction. Dayton's, along with three local heavyweights—Honeywell, Northwest Bancorporation, and General Mills— eventually banded together to create a school to collectively train their executives and managers. The "Four Company Program" was unique—no other city in America offered anything comparable—and proved cost-efficient.

"Mom and dad and the kids all piled into the car, they went out to this big store, and they could spend several hours there."

—MARC LEVINSON, Author and Historian

DISCOUNT RETAIL

Creating a discount store had been percolating in the minds of the Dayton brothers, and in the collective minds of other department store executives across the United States. Credit Eugene Ferkauf for bringing discount to the forefront of everyone's attention. Ferkauf, who hailed from Brooklyn, understood the postwar consumer better than anybody: they wanted to buy things for their homes, and they wanted value in what they purchased. He opened E.J. Korvette with the idea of discounting merchandise far more than anybody had ever dared.

His efforts, however, were complicated by fair-trade laws—specifically the 1937 Miller-Tydings amendment to the Sherman Anti-Trust Act. Congress had passed the amendment to empower the manufacturers of name-brand merchandise, who were now able to force retailers to sell their products at the suggested retail price. The idea had been to protect small store owners through a practice known as price maintenance.

" Ferkauf, who hailed from Brooklyn, understood the postwar consumer better than anybody: they wanted to buy things for their homes, and they wanted value in what they purchased. He opened E.J. Korvette with the idea of discounting merchandise far more than anybody had ever dared.

The intrepid Ferkauf navigated the restriction by establishing Korvette as a membership organization and not a retail store. Doing so allowed Ferkauf to persuade distributors to sell him wholesale merchandise at a discount. Becoming a Korvette member was hardly an exclusive affiliation: Korvette passed out membership cards from the pavement in front of his store. Members would then enter the store with their card in hand to shop for discounted merchandise. Once inside, shoppers would find products piled haphazardly from soup to nuts, a virtually nonexistent sales staff, and a spartan décor—all items were priced to move.

Ferkauf followed the fundamentals of operating a successful business, which cut out the fat—there were no frills, and he was able to count on a high volume of sales to make up for low profit margins. And he was a master at using a loss-leader: for example, he'd stock select hard-to-get appliances in his store and price them at cost. Little surprise he sold the items as fast as he put them up for sale. Eventually, he began to dip his beak, taking small markups of 5 to 20 percent. Since his competitors continued to have markups of 40 percent and higher, customers continued to shop at Korvette.[1]

Nobody liked a boat rocker, and clearly, Ferkauf rocked the boat, prompting other retailers to whine to their suppliers that they needed to quit fortifying Ferkhauf's stores. When the suppliers gave in, Ferkauf simply used alternate brands. Eventually, the suppliers that had ceded to the pressure realized they were missing Korvette's volume orders and begged forgiveness, often offering healthy discounts to adequately express their sincerity.[2]

> " Becoming a Korvette member was hardly an exclusive affiliation: Korvette passed out membership cards from the pavement in front of his store. Members would then enter the store with their card in hand to shop for discounted merchandise. Once inside, shoppers would find products piled haphazardly from soup to nuts, a virtually nonexistent sales staff, and a spartan décor—all items were priced to move.

Jack Schwadron, merchandising vice president of Korvette's, addressed the store's immense success in an August 30, 1961, interview with the (Camden, New Jersey) *Courier-Post*. "It isn't magic," Schwadron said. "We haven't pulled any rabbits out of the hat. It's a very simple formula. Namely this: we don't tack costly services on to the price of the merchandise. We have service available if you need it. The same applies to delivery. We don't deliver unless the item is too big to be carried, but there again, you pay the delivery charge. Another thing. Operational expenses are kept to a minimum. Add to that our tremendous buying power and you have a few of the reasons that Korvette has gone so far so fast. But that isn't all. One of the main reasons is our strict merchandising policy of only stocking top quality, brand name merchandise and more of it in a wider assortment. Our price lines on this merchandise run broader too, from low to medium to medium to high than the traditional department store. In other words, our departments are much more complete."[3]

As author David Halberstam wrote in his book *The Fifties*: "Gene had a simple philosophy: He was going to take discounting further than it had ever been taken before. If [Ferkauf] could make a one-dollar profit selling a refrigerator, he said at the beginning, then he would do it, because he could make a million dollars by selling a million of them."[4]

If [Ferkauf] could make a one-dollar profit selling a refrigerator, he said at the beginning, then he would do it, because he could make a million dollars by selling a million of them.

The Era of the Big-Box Store

Ferkauf had used $4,000 to begin his business in 1948, and by mid-July of 1962, he had opened seventeen stores in the Northeast with projected sales of $230 million that year.[5] America's growing suburbs had caught his attention. They were fertile ground for discount retailers to infiltrate—and this ushered in the era of the "big-box" store. Typically, a big-box store has a large amount of floor space, a large variety of items available for sale, and a location in a suburban area. Big-box stores could offer lower prices because they purchased products in high volume and had easily accessible parking lots.

"Everybody had to have a car because the big-box was sitting out in a parking lot somewhere," said historian and author Marc Levinson. "The big-box made shopping into a family experience. Mom and dad and the kids all piled into the car, they went out to this big store, and they could spend several hours there because there was, by the standards of the day, an enormous amount of merchandise. Now, you've got to give people a little sense of scale. We're talking about stores that were gigantic for their time, and that meant they might have about 50,000 square feet of space. If you go into a typical Walmart Supercenter today, it's perhaps four times that size. So 'big' is relative, but for its day, 1962, these stores were quite large."[6] Further, the laws that once prevented big retailers from receiving volume discounts began to go away in the 1950s, eliminating an obstacle for discount retailing. Savvy retailers could see the way the wind had begun to blow and acted accordingly. Dayton's was among the retailers opting to find out more about the discount market, where low prices, high volume, and quick turnover were king.

Hoping to strengthen relationships with consumers, the Dayton brothers were itching to start their own mass-market discount chain that catered to value-oriented shoppers. The alternative was to sit back and watch other stores enter the market. Some industry experts deemed the idea of Dayton's entering the discount retail market as risky. The company already held a dominant position as a department store retailer, so why change their identity? During a monthly management meeting in 1960, the brothers heard a compelling talk from Ira Hayes of the National Cash Register Company. Hayes addressed discount merchandising and offered glowing descriptions of the long lines of customers waiting to buy discounted merchandise at New England's old textile mills. He stressed that a consumer demand existed.[7]

> " Hoping to strengthen relationships with consumers, the Dayton brothers were itching to start their own mass-market discount chain that catered to value-oriented shoppers. The alternative was to sit back and watch other stores enter the market.

Dayton's employed 40 percent margins in its stores.[8] The margins at discount stores would be well below that figure. But the concept of selling more for less rather than selling less for more was not totally unfamiliar to the Dayton brothers. They had experience offering lower prices. Dayton's Downstairs

Store had established itself as a prosperous, low-priced option in the basement of the original downtown Dayton's. Thus, they weren't considering an area of retail with which they were totally unfamiliar. An ad that ran in the *Minneapolis Star*[9] touted what customers could expect at Dayton's Downstairs Store as follows:

EXTRA LOW PRICES—Our expert comparison shoppers scour the whole city checking prices so that we can assure you of lower prices!

EXTRA WIDE SELECTIONS—Thousands of items in a huge assortment of colors, sizes and styles arranged for easy selection and comparison.

EXTRA FINE QUALITY—For over 50 years, Dayton's Downstairs Store has made it a policy to have fine quality merchandise for its customers.

EXTRA SHOPPING CONVENIENCES—Shop for family and home needs on one floor with the assistance of our capable, friendly salespeople!

EXTRA SERVICES—Buy with confidence . . . unsatisfactory merchandise may be returned. Use Dayton's phone or mail service. No charge for delivery of items over $3 in the metropolitan area!

EXTRA VALUE ITEMS—Found on this page are typical of the values you'll find every day in Dayton's Downstairs Store. "The Store of Lower Prices."

Thus, the Dayton brothers were familiar with the concept of discount, just not at a large scale.

John Geisse helped nurture the idea of Dayton's opening a discount chain. Geisse had graduated from the US Naval Academy in 1941, then served as a lieutenant commander of the USS *Tuscaloosa* during World War II.[10] He served in the Pacific and Atlantic in World War II, and participated in the Normandy invasion.[11] After rising to the rank of lieutenant commander, Geisse left the navy and decided that Minneapolis looked like an attractive area to live. Dayton's hired him as a buyer of drugs, stationery, and notions.[12] At one point, Geisse was a buyer and a divisional merchandise manager in Dayton's Downstairs Store.[13] He claimed the idea for Target was his.

Geisse had prepared a thorough report illuminating the pros and cons of discount stores and pushed Dayton's accordingly. Influenced by a University of Denver research paper on retailing formats and armed with his knowledge gained from working in the retail industry, Geisse concluded that Dayton's would be missing a golden opportunity if it did not enter the arena—an arena that did not conflict with the department store's customer. On July 8, 1961, the Dayton family announced that they planned to form a chain of discount stores in the Minneapolis–St. Paul area and, eventually, in other locations in cities in the Upper Midwest states.[14]

"Target Stores was my idea originally, and I had decided in 1960 to leave the Dayton Company and set up my own operation offering brand name, quality merchandise to the middle-income shopper," said Geisse in a 1970 interview with the *St. Louis Post-Dispatch*. "Then the Dayton management pointed out that I would need capital—something they had. So I agreed to stay with Dayton and develop a discount subsidiary provided I could have an equity interest."[15]

Geisse's lack of capital likely stemmed from the fact that he and his wife, Mary, had ten children—five boys and five girls.[16] In agreeing to stay with Dayton, he was given a 6 percent share of Target Stores[17] and he was named vice president and general merchandise manager of Target Stores, Inc.

Douglas J. Dayton, vice president and director of Dayton's, was chosen to head the new corporation, which would have no connection to Dayton's department stores.[18] Target planned to differentiate itself from other discounters by offering quality merchandise at low margins, which they were able to do because they planned to cut expenses.[19] "We would much rather do this than trumpet dramatic price cuts on cheap merchandise," Douglas Dayton said.[20]

The new chain's offerings included home furnishings, clothing and accessories, and a discount supermarket with an emphasis on "quick and convenient" shopping. Geisse said stores would solve the need for distributing certain types of medium-to-better-quality merchandise, which could be bought more quickly—and at lower prices—from shopping racks than it could in department stores.[21] Douglas Dayton explained that they had executed their due diligence in their studies of current and future trends in retail distribution and concluded: "We have become convinced that if we are able to continue to offer a complete shopping service to the customers in our trade area, we should undertake further expansion through the addition of discount stores."[22]

"We will be merely
buying what you want,
applying a very low
mark-up, and selling at
low prices—but very,
very competitive prices."

—DONALD DAYTON

CHAPTER FIVE

TARGET COMES TO LIFE

S tewart K. Widdess, Dayton's director of publicity, had the duty of creating a name for the new entity, one that would not confuse shoppers with the parent department-store chain. Widdess and his staff mulled over two hundred possibilities before deciding on "Target," along with the store's iconic red-and-white bullseye symbol. Widdess explained that "as a marksman's goal is to hit the center bullseye, the new store would do much the same in terms of retail goods, services, commitment to the community, price, value and overall experience."[1]

Target's first print ad campaigns carried the tagline: "Aim straight for Target discount stores." While Target's logo has evolved over the years, it has remained close to the original, which featured the brand name in black lettering over a red and white bullseye with three red circles and two white circles. The new company was incorporated under the name "Target Stores, Inc."

" Widdess explained that "as a marksman's goal is to hit the center bullseye, the new store would do much the same in terms of retail goods, services, commitment to the community, price, value and overall experience." Target's first print ad campaigns carried the tagline: "Aim straight for Target discount stores."

Dayton Corporation earmarked $4 million to start four discount stores in the following Minnesota locations: St. Paul, Crystal, St. Louis Park, and Duluth. However, a glitch prevented the St. Paul location from coming to fruition, so the Daytons were forced to find a new location. They settled on a partially built structure in the St. Paul suburb of Roseville and finished off the building. In May of 1962 the first Target store opened. Seventy-five departments fit neatly inside the 82,500-square-foot building at 1515 West County Road B. They included a grocery store, a shoe department, a hat department, and even a dry cleaner.

While department stores had previously tried to deal with discount stores by highlighting service, variety, and fashion, and by competing with them directly—offering certain items at reduced prices—Donald Dayton noted that Dayton's would remain the same. "We subscribe to the spectrum theory of retailing," Dayton said. "At one end of the spectrum will be the top-quality, fashion-right department store. At the other end will be the discount store."[2]

Thus, Dayton's would continue to offer large and complete assortments of merchandise, with strong emphasis on fashion in all categories and full department store customer services, such as credit, delivery options, and courteous salespeople.

Separate but Equal

Target's main offices were located in the Dayton Corporation's headquarters, but everything else about Target operated separately: it had separate buyers and separate computers. This separation proved essential to Target's success. "Our independence from Dayton's [proved critical]," Doug Dayton said. "[Other discount stores] did not have enough independence from their department-store parents to do it. Ken [Dayton], as Dayton's general merchandising manager was working to keep Dayton's merchandise out of discount, while Target was battling to get in. . . . We didn't think for more than a moment, for instance, about whether to share a mainframe between the two operations. We each had our own."[3]

Target's opening in 1962 coincided with the openings of several other large discount stores across the country, including Kmart—which opened its first store in Garden City, Michigan, on March 1, 1962—and Walmart, which opened its first store in Rogers, Arkansas, on July 2, 1962. Target added additional stores that first year with locations in Minneapolis–St. Paul suburbs Knollwood, Duluth, and Crystal.

Discount stores had been punctuating the retail landscape at great speed: the year prior, F.W. Woolworth Co. entered the arena by opening Woolco Co., while Allied Stores, Corp.—the parent firm of Donaldson's in Minneapolis—had set up its Almart division. Target sought to differentiate itself from the competition by projecting itself as an upscale discount retailer. According to the *New York Times*, John Geisse "was credited with the concept of adapting better quality merchandise to the discount format of reduced prices, large open stock and essentially self-service shopping."[4]

Target made the decision that they could discount their merchandise at any level, so they went with the highest and opted to establish the chain as the quality discounter.[5] As a Target ad in May of 1962 announced: "Here's news for people whose taste runs to the better things in life. A new kind of discount store for people who demand and understand quality . . . [offering] better lines of everything from groceries to high fashion. And all at EVERYDAY DISCOUNT PRICES."[6]

In addition to offering higher quality staples at reduced, competitive prices, Target opened with several department store features that further differentiated them within the market of discount retailers, including money-back guarantees, credit, and exchange privileges.

> " In addition to offering higher quality staples at reduced, competitive prices, Target opened with several department store features that further differentiated them within the market of discount retailers, including money-back guarantees, credit, and exchange privileges.

Target clearly carried the markings of a discount store—they just didn't embrace the "discount" categorization and instead advertised the store's merchandise as "medium-priced."

"To be a discount operation, there has to be somebody else's price or a general price that you're discounting," Donald Dayton said. "We won't just be trying to knock someone else's price out. We will be merely buying what you want, applying a very low mark-up, and selling at low prices—but very, very competitive prices."[7]

Target lost money initially, which prompted a more conservative approach toward expansion. But it turned out that the losses in fact stemmed from an overstocking problem, so Target held a discount sale to rid themselves of the extra inventory. Target purchased a mainframe computer to help clear the overstock.[8] "When we were thinking about computers, we went to National Cash Register for advice," said Douglas Dayton in *The Birth of Target.* "We got a great big IBM with a chair in the middle. After we got that, our store registers printed out sales on punch tape. The tape could run out; the system wasn't elegant. We'd have 25,000 feet of tape to process, but the Target group thought it was radar."[9]

Gaining their footing convinced the Dayton brothers that they could move forward to open a Target in Bloomington, Minnesota. That store reached its sales goal of $10 million in 1965.[10]

Customers had immediately recognized a difference between Target and other discount stores. This had everything to do with the decision to continue establishing Target as a more upscale brand—and it even earned the store's chic nickname, "Tarzhay." "We surprised 'em, because they had such low expectations for a discount store," Douglas Dayton said.[11]

Two new stores were opened in Denver in 1966, and by the end of the year, the seven Target stores had $60 million in sales. Additional Targets were opened in Minnesota in 1967.

> **" Customers had immediately recognized a difference between Target and other discount stores. This had everything to do with the decision to continue establishing Target as a more upscale brand—and it even earned the store's chic nickname, "Tarzhay." "We surprised 'em, because they had such low expectations for a discount store."**

The brothers continued their practice of meeting for Saturday lunches to discuss various aspects of the business, including questions about the future. None of the sixteen Daytons that comprised the family's fourth generation showed any inclination to join the business, which meant the brothers had to decide how the company should proceed: they could either sell out and become a major national company, maintain status quo and delay the question, or grow the company nationally.

The brothers examined the advantages of remaining a private company against the advantages of going public. Going public made the most sense. It would create an influx of cash that would better equip the company to make acquisitions for future growth. "We carefully analyzed all the things that were necessary to form a growth company," Kenneth Dayton told the

New York Times. "We knew we had to go public, and we made that decision many years before we actually went public. In fact, we published two annual reports as a private company to give ourselves the discipline of being public."[12] The company first released a report of net profit and sales figures in 1964 and continued the practice the following year.

It was clear that Dayton's needed to expand its board. In typical Dayton brother fashion, they looked hard at what they wanted and took a proactive approach, bringing in executives in the Minneapolis–St. Paul area. Each had vast experience and fresh ideas for ways to improve the Dayton Company. Invitations to join the board were extended to Stephen F. Keating, president of Honeywell, Inc.; Robert J. Keith, chair of the Pillsbury Company; David M. Lilly, president of Tory Manufacturing Corporation; and Phillip H. Nason, president of the First National Bank of Saint Paul.

"Don and Bruce came to see me and said they were looking for professional people to be on their board," Lilly said. "Bruce Dayton and I had been directors of Frist National Bank of Minneapolis, and by chance we had attended American Management Association classes on professional management at the same time. While our companies were different, our businesses were the same—satisfying customer needs. . . . I knew the other outside directors. Keating and Nason were also directors of Toro. The Daytons and The Dayton Company were well thought of; they were determined not to be anything but professional; they never were a family taking advantage of the family company by virtue of their positions as owners. Even when they came up with a formula for executive compensation, they didn't take all of what they offered to others."[13]

The company simulated shareholder meetings and even went so far as to hire an actor to behave like a nuisance. They also worked to figure out a way for the company's management to be afforded opportunities to buy shares prior to going public.[14]

At a special shareholders meeting on September 6, 1967, the Dayton Company changed its name to Dayton Corporation,[15] which consisted of five divisions—Dayton's Department Stores; Target Stores; B. Dalton, Bookseller; Dayton's Jewelers; and the Dayton Development Company.

Going Public

The Dayton Corporation went public on October 18, 1967, when 450,000 common stocks were offered at $34 a share. The offering represented 15 percent of the outstanding shares of common stock; Dayton family members held the balance.[16]

The Dayton brothers wanted to continue expanding Target, and going public aided their pursuit. Target moved into St. Louis in 1968—the chain now had a total of eleven stores—and looked to extend its reach into other new markets.[17]

❝ The Dayton brothers wanted to continue expanding Target, and going public aided their pursuit. Target moved into St. Louis in 1968—the chain now had a total of eleven stores—and looked to extend its reach into other new markets.

While discount stores such as Target thrived, traditional department stores struggled—particularly those located in downtown areas, such as J. L. Hudson of Detroit. J. L. Hudson Company of Detroit owned J. L. Hudson in downtown Detroit, along with the branches in Michigan and Ohio. The stores had long dominated the Detroit market, but profits had begun to dwindle. Changing times—including increased migration to the suburbs and civil rights unrest in the summer of 1967—contributed to Hudson's woes, as did the deaths of three of the four owners. Finding itself in a precarious position, J.L. Hudson struck a deal with the Dayton Corporation.

Dayton Corporation purchased J.L. Hudson Co., Detroit in May of 1969. The acquisition brought the nation's largest independently owned department store operation into the fold and ultimately gave birth to Dayton Hudson Corporation, which became Dayton Corporation's new name in 1971.

Hudson's became a wholly owned subsidiary of Dayton Hudson, a retailer composed of Target and five major department store chains that had combined sales exceeding $800 million. At the time of the acquisition, it was the fourteenth largest non-food retailer in the United States. When Dayton Corporation's real estate company became Dayton Hudson Properties, it picked up $100 million in real estate.[18]

"We were trying to find out if customers would buy the same merchandise strictly because of price. The answer was yes."

—**SAM WALTON** on the first Walmart

CHAPTER SIX

THE COMPETITION

Kmart and Walmart were Target's competition from their beginnings in 1962. Each came into being through the efforts of retail pioneers Harry Cunningham and Sam Walton, who guided Kmart and Walmart, respectively. To say the least, they were formidable opponents. All could swim in the deep end of the discount-store pool, and each sought to find their own niche.

Cunningham's talents became apparent early in his career with S.S. Kresge Co., a nationally known "five-and-dime" store that sold inexpensive merchandise. Working as a store manager, he began having clerks fill out blue cards with customer requests. Customer service wasn't new to retailing, but institutionalizing such a practice across all stores was unique. Cunningham's policy helped the chain double its sales.

Cunningham had vaulted to become Kresge's superintendent of stores by 1947. Once again, he brought new ideas to his job such as implementing a central-checkout model, like the ones he'd observed in many supermarkets.

By 1957, Cunningham had risen to a general vice president position with Kresge and was sent on a two-year mission to gather the pulse of the company's stores, Kresge's competitors, and the customers they sought to satisfy. The mission saw him log well over two hundred thousand travel miles, and convinced Cunningham that the five-and-dime model in small spaces—like those of Kresge's stores—had grown stagnant and had dismal prospects for the future. Cunningham praised E. J. Korvette's model of large discount stores with high-volume turnover, low profit margins, and cheap prices—a theme that played well in the suburbs as their populations swelled and Americans grew increasingly obsessed with hopping into their automobiles and going to stores with large parking lots to shop.

> By 1957, Cunningham had risen to a general vice president position with Kresge and was sent on a two-year mission to gather the pulse of the company's stores, Kresge's competitors, and the customers they sought to satisfy. The mission saw him log well over two hundred thousand travel miles, and convinced Cunningham that the five-and-dime model in small spaces—like those of Kresge's stores—had grown stagnant and had dismal prospects for the future.

The Launch of Kmart

Cunningham's initial report, along with his suggestions for the future—which included transitioning to a discount store format—met deaf ears with Kresge's board. However, when he became the company's CEO in 1960, he received approval to implement his plan and move into discount. S.S. Kresge Co. dedicated $80 million in merchandise and leases for Kmart, their new big-box retailer. Kmart launched in 1962 with eighteen stores—which brought $483 million in corporate sales that year. Following Cunningham's guidance, Kmart relied on lowered prices and reduced inventory, going against the grain by offering permanent discounts on national brands.

They were able to reduce prices because they reduced overhead. Stores were built on cheap property close to suburban highways and had fewer floor staff, which encouraged customers to serve themselves by perusing the merchandise that filled the racks and tables. High-end retail services such as gift wrapping and home delivery were not available, but customers did not have to go from store to store to purchase items because of Kmart's wide variety of stock. Brand-name merchandise could be bought under one roof at discounted prices. And Cunningham brought back the blue-card idea to form the "Blue Light Special"—an alert about daily specials passed on to customers via flashing blue lights accompanied by the iconic cry, "Attention: Kmart shoppers . . ."

By 1966, Kmart had 162 stores. Combined sales from those stores and the 753 Kresge stores exceeded $1 billion. Fully confident in its Kmart stores, S.S. Kresge astounded the retail world by boldly opening 271 Kmart locations in 1976.[1]

Because almost 95 percent of S. S. Kresge Company sales were generated by Kmart stores, the company changed its name to Kmart Corporation in 1977.[2] A decade later, the company sold the remaining Kresge stores to fully concentrate on discount merchandising with Kmart, which had expanded to over a thousand stores that generated $8.4 billion in sales, making them the second largest retailer in the country behind Sears.[3]

 Kmart had expanded to over a thousand stores that generated $8.4 billion in sales, making them the second largest retailer in the country behind Sears.

Walmart's Beginnings

In 1940, Sam Walton was hired as a sales trainee in a Des Moines, Iowa, J.C. Penney, where the commissions he earned identified him as a gifted salesman. Military service interrupted his retail career when he got drafted into the army in 1942, where he worked in the Army Intelligence Corps as a communications officer. Once his obligation was complete, he pieced together enough money from his own personal savings and a loan from his father-in-law to buy a variety store in Newport, Arkansas.

The store, a Ben Franklin, was a franchise of the Butler Brothers chain. Walton priced his goods below other area retailers and worked hard, tripling sales within a five-year period and making his store the top Ben Franklin in a six-state area. Walton's landlord had a retail background, and he was inspired by Walton's success to attempt to buy the store for his son. When Walton would not sell, the landlord declined to renew his lease and bought out the store's stock and furnishings for $50,000. Despite the fact that his life was upturned, Walton believed he'd received a fair price and moved on with a business lesson in his back pocket.[4] In the future, he would never again sign a lease without a renewal option, and he also wouldn't hand over 5 percent of his sales as part of his rent.

Walton uprooted his family and moved to Bentonville, Arkansas, in 1950, where he found a desirable building on the town square and opened Walton's Five & Dime. This time around, he came away with a ninety-nine-year lease, and his retail acumen and work ethic continued to pay off. Hardly content to operate just one store no matter how well it did, Walton used profits and loans to parlay his success into opening more stores. Ten years later, he and his brother, James, had become Ben Franklin's largest franchisee, owning fifteen stores throughout Arkansas, Kansas, and Missouri.[5]

For all of his success, Walton wasn't pleased with the fruits of his labor. Profits were unsatisfactory. He decided he needed to go in another direction, one that would see him own big stores that priced merchandise low enough to undercut the competition. High sales volumes would compensate for the lower prices. Geographically, he saw his stores benefiting small towns. Walton approached the Ben Franklin executives for backing. They didn't like the idea of cutting their wholesale margins to enable him to charge the prices he wanted to offer. But Walton's conviction did not waver. He mortgaged his home and borrowed. With $72,000 in his coffers, Walton opened the first Walmart in 1962 in Rogers, Arkansas, a small city in the Ozarks near Bentonville.[6]

Walton described that first store in detail in his autobiography: "The store was only 12,000 square feet, and had an eight-foot ceiling and a concrete floor, with bare-boned wooden plank fixtures. Sterling [a competitor] had a huge variety store in downtown Harrison, with tile on the floor, nice lights, really good fixtures, and good presentations. Ours was just barely put together—highly promotional, truly ugly, heavy with merchandise—but for 20% less than the competition. We were trying to find out if customers in a town of 6,000 people would come to our kind of a barn and buy the same merchandise strictly because of price. The answer was yes."[7]

Rural America loved Walton's stores. Sales and growth reflected their popularity. "I had no vision of the scope of what I would start," Walton said. "But I always had confidence that as long as we did our work well and were good to our customers, there would be no limit to us."[8]

Walmart had expanded to twenty-four stores by 1967 and had $13 million in annual sales. By 1970, they had thirty-eight locations with $44 million in annual sales. However, further expansion was not immediately feasible due to the chain's debt. Walton was able to remedy the lack of cash in the fall of 1970 when he took Walmart public, retaining 61 percent ownership.[9]

The influx of dollars equipped Walmart with enough capital to expand to fifty-seven stores by the end of 1972, and to continue to grow aggressively in the years that followed. By the end of the 1970s, Walton had 276 stores, 21,000 employees, and $1 billion in annual sales.[10]

In 1983, Walton introduced Sam's Wholesale Clubs, massive supercenters that targeted small-business owners and those wanting to buy merchandise in bulk. Again, Walton hit the jackpot. Walmart improved to the third-largest retailer in the United States in 1987; Sears and Kmart still held the top spots.

> In 1983, Walton introduced Sam's Wholesale Clubs, massive supercenters that targeted small-business owners and those wanting to buy merchandise in bulk. Again, Walton hit the jackpot. Walmart improved to the third-largest retailer in the United States in 1987; Sears and Kmart still held the top spots.

The Slow and Steady Expansion of Target

At the other end of the spectrum in comparison to the rapid expansions of Kmart and Walmart, the Dayton family took a prudent approach for how Target proceeded. The May Department Stores Company, located in St. Louis, hoped to tap into some of Target's magic. John Geisse, who resigned from Target in August 1968, was hired to become the president of Venture, May's fledgling discount retail store, effective September 1, 1968.[11]

"John went from Target [to the May Company] with the rolled-up blueprints of the chain under his arm—and the first Venture store was identical in layout," said Norm McMillan, a former Target executive. "He was disappointed he wasn't named president of [Target]."[12]

Geisse allowed that his move to the May Company created "some static" due to the May operations in Denver and St. Louis, where Target had stores.[13]

Seven other top Target executives followed Geisse to May.[14]

Geisse took concepts to Venture that had worked at Target. "We intend to offer high quality merchandise that will appeal to the middle and upper income suburban shopper," said Geisse in an interview with the *St. Louis Post-Dispatch.* "Beyond this we have set up a system of information feedback that keeps us in touch with what it is that shoppers want."[15]

Geisse also leaned on an in-depth customer profile developed before Target Stores launched in St. Louis in 1968. The profile that evolved from that study showed that discount store shoppers generally had large families, were younger than shoppers who did their shopping at department stores, liked leisure-time activities, and were above average in education and income.[16]

Under Geisse's guidance, Venture would open two St. Louis stores in 1970.

William A. Hodder had joined Dayton's from IBM in May 1966 to become the director of organizational planning and development, and once Geisse departed, he moved into Geisse's role as Target's senior vice president and general merchandise manager in August 1968. That December, when Douglas J. Dayton—who had served as Target president since the beginning—moved to the role of senior vice president of Dayton Corporation, Hodder was immediately named Target president.

Geisse continued to excel elsewhere. In 1982, he founded the Wholesale Club of Indianapolis, and by 1990, he'd built it to a twenty-plus store chain with $650 million in annual sales. Walmart acquired the Wholesale Club in 1990 in exchange for Walmart stock and cash worth $21 per share to Wholesale Club's existing shareholders, making the Wholesale Club worth approximately $170 million. The stores were incorporated into Walmart's Sam's Club chain.[17]

Geisse's exact contribution to Target remains unclear; however, he played an integral role in the company's history. In light of McMillan's comment that Geisse had been disappointed that he had not been named president and the timing of Hodder's succession, it appears as if the decision had been made months earlier when Geisse was still working for Target. What's certain is that Geisse's departure—coupled with the fact that he took several key management people with him—hurt Target, and that it triggered an era of management problems.[18]

"Business is not complicated, but many executives try to make it a mystical thing, but it's not."

—STEVEN PISTNER, Target President

CHAPTER SEVEN

STRUGGLES AND SOLUTIONS

When the Dayton Corporation went public in 1967, there were nine Target stores, four Dayton's Department Stores, and a handful of jewelry and bookstores. Together they produced approximately $265 million in sales.[1] But the company hardly experienced smooth sailing.

J. L. Hudson's had been a family-owned department store, and had not focused on a quality metric: sales per square foot. "They wanted to be the biggest and the finest," Kenneth Dayton said. "And they were." Hudson's had plush surroundings where they weren't necessary and "360,000-square-foot stores where 250,000 would have done the job."[2] Additional problems included a lack of merchandising expertise, inventory control, and buying plans.

Edwin Roberts became Hudson's president in 1972, bringing along a reputation as a solid merchandiser. He was joined by a Dayton Hudson controller and a top-notch merchandiser. The trio cleaned up the mess, reducing costs and ridding

Hudson's inventory of unprofitable, low-margin product lines. Their efforts helped it become Dayton Hudson's top profit producer by the end of 1973—a period in which Target experienced problems of its own.

In deference to Dayton Hudson's conservative strategy toward expansion, six Target stores were opened in Texas and Oklahoma in 1969 and seven stores were added in 1970, bringing the total to twenty-four stores with $200 million in sales. By the end of 1972, that number had increased to forty-six stores.

Of the twenty-one stores opened between May of 1971 and June of 1972, nineteen had belonged to Arlan's, a struggling department store chain with locations in Nebraska, Oklahoma, Iowa, Illinois, and Colorado. Remerchandising and remodeling those stores became a cash drain. Gross profits for Dayton Hudson Corporation's low-margin group, of which Target made up more than 80 percent, dropped to $13 million in 1973 from $18 million in 1971.[3]

Flaws in the Target Design

Kenneth Dayton allowed that the company's ambitious approach had proved costly. He rationalized that the "market overshot us" making "unrealistic" the company's expectations.[4]

Target's merchandising system suddenly showed flaws as well.

Serving a larger geographical footprint than Minneapolis and its surrounding areas, Target struggled to stock items that fit the climate and buying habits of those in different geographical areas. Dayton cited having walleye lures in Houston stores as an example. Fishing for walleye in the Gulf of Mexico would have been pointless since walleye do not exist there.[5]

Target decentralized merchandising to take into account local considerations, but further refinements were needed. The chain clearly had lost its way. Some stores were found in disarray, having taken it upon themselves to decorate with their own look. Others demonstrated low employee accountability and had unacceptable store conditions—including poor merchandise placement, dirty floors, and out-of-date inventory. These stores strayed from the promise of the Target brand, which was supposed to deliver a quality shopping experience.

> **The chain clearly had lost its way. Some stores were found in disarray, having taken it upon themselves to decorate with their own look. Others demonstrated low employee accountability and had unacceptable store conditions—including poor merchandise placement, dirty floors, and out-of-date inventory. These stores strayed from the promise of the Target brand, which was supposed to deliver a quality shopping experience.**

On March 23, 1973, Dayton Hudson Corporation reassigned Hodder as the senior vice president of specialty, and they named Stephen L. Pistner Target president. Target "had lost thrust and direction, and it had grown too fast," Pistner said. "There were too few qualified executives to carry its growth."[6]

Pistner's experience was eclectic and included a stint selling adding machines door-to-door. He gained a reputation for finding success through his work at Electronics Associates, where he ascended from sales manager to president of the St. Paul electronics wholesaler. Pistner then bought the company, renamed it Team Electronics, and transformed the wholesaler into a top-notch retail operation. That success had enticed Dayton Hudson into buying Team Electronics in 1970.

Because of his IBM background, Hodder tended to rely on technology to find solutions, preferring computer readouts to individuals. In Pistner, the Daytons found Hodder's polar opposite: a leader who didn't mind getting his hands dirty, liked working with people, and carried an unprecedented fearlessness. "In effect, I'm not afraid," Pistner said. "I have a great deal of faith in what I do."[7]

Thus began the Target turnaround.

Pistner "has a powerful voice and he drills you with his eyeballs," said Norman McMillan, who worked in a number of positions at Target. "He has a lust for words. He laughs harder than anybody I know and yells louder than anybody I know. When he hears a good idea, he doesn't just nod his head, he'll stand up and shout, 'That's the best idea I ever heard.'"[8]

According to Alan Pennington, Dayton Hudson vice president of planning, Pistner's "great strengths are being able to put the right people together in the right way and to look at an entire business from a strategic point of view with the customer."[9]

Described as colorful, immodest, and aggressive, Pistner was also recognized as a motivator. In a 1977 story that ran in the *Des Moines Tribune,* an anonymous Pistner associate called him "an extremely effective guy." "While he's hard to work with and live with, he has a positive effect on an organization overall," the associate said. "He's extremely intelligent and articulate and he's extremely persuasive. He's the kind of guy that could sell refrigerators to Eskimos."[10]

Inside Pistner's office, a needlepoint pillow displayed a battlefield that featured a dragon staring at an empty suit of armor. Etched underneath were the words, "Things my mother never told me. . . . Sometimes the dragon wins."[11] Pistner wasn't afraid to try to slay the dragon.

Pistner Makes Some Changes

Three weeks into his position with Target, Pistner was told by a Dayton Hudson consultant that he was wasting his time trying to get Target back on its feet. "The leader of this consulting company came in with a smirk on his face and told me in effect, that I was dead and that the discount concept was dead," Pistner said. "Needless to say, that firm never did another lick of work for Dayton Hudson."[12]

Pistner began to evaluate what was needed to revamp the troubled company, a process he believed required a combination of studying what Target had done in the past and "asking a series of questions that help you understand the truth of where the business is at the moment."[13] Seeking the truth often illuminated the real competency levels of company executives—and it also revealed the ones he could trust. "You make judgment calls about people," Pistner said. "There, I have a high level of accuracy. There, I'm at my best."[14]

An unnamed source in a 1977 *Des Moines Tribune*[15] article credited Pistner for making Target "much more responsive to consumers."[16] In meetings held with Target's ten top executives, Pistner asked them to explain what they perceived to be Target's problem.[17] "I was told the company had too [many] expenses and that consumers wouldn't buy more," Pistner said. "They said we had to wait to see the trends reverse themselves rather than asking how can the business reverse itself." Seven of those ten executives were let go.[18]

Pistner revamped Target's merchandising system, making sure the company stayed in tune with consumer trends, and he put in operating and expense controls.[19] Growth was scaled back to sharpen the focus on improving every Target store. Pistner found support in Kenneth A. Macke, a senior vice president who joined Pistner's effort to try and reinvigorate Target. Both stressed the importance of getting back to the basics. Pistner believed that executives rarely went to the right people to seek solutions. "Too few executives don't realize that problems can be solved by talking with people who work in it. Business is not complicated, but many executives try to make it a mystical thing, but it's not."[20]

Instead, he listened to consumers to uncover areas that needed to be addressed. "Consumers will tell you what's right and what's wrong, and they'll tell you in five minutes flat what they don't like."[21]

It soon became clear that there were problems at the front of stores, where, customers told him, confusion reigned. Pistner called in a group of cashiers composed entirely of women and asked them to come up with a list of reasons why the front of the stores had grown so shoddy. Afraid for their jobs, the women asked for—and received—Pistner's assurance that they would remain anonymous. They then handed Pistner ten suggestions for improvement, which were given to store managers who were told to follow them. It wasn't long before the operations at the front of Target's stores were running smoothly.[22]

"We found out the entrances were too narrow, so we reopened the doors and we repositioned the place where the checkout lanes were," Pistner said. "We changed the whole setup in the front."[23]

Macke, like Pistner, employed a hands-on approach, like going into a Target Store and ramming a shopping cart into a display. The visual illustrated the problems with cluttered aisles.[24] "The customers of Target say they want cleaner, wider aisles, and it's Target's job to provide them," Macke said. "My job is to be our toughest customer."[25]

A Guide for Growth

In 1974, at a company retreat at a Minneapolis hotel,[26] Norm McMillan, Target's vice president for strategic planning, was tasked to lead a team of executives to come up with a vision for the company.[27] From that exercise, a comprehensive mission statement known as "Decision Guides"[28] was developed, and distributed to employees, so they could follow for guidance. That mission statement came to be known as "Guides for Growth."[29] At the end of the seventeen-page document, a summary for Guides for Growth is presented under a heading of, "This is what we will stand for; it is how Target intends to grow," and proceeded with the following:

- Target Respects the People Who Shop Its Stores
- Target Is a Store for Young Families
- Target Is an Honest-Dealing Store
- Target Has Dominance in the Merchandise Customers Want Most
- Target Is a Trend Merchant

- Target Sells Higher Quality Merchandise
- Target Puts Its Name Only on Top Quality Merchandise
- Target's Pricing Is Balanced
- Target Is a Chain
- Target Is a Mass Merchant
- Target Is a Self-Service Mass Merchant
- Target Matches Service to Customer Expectations
- Target Is a Chain with Some Specialized Businesses
- Target Is Committed to Low Expenses
- Target Uses Management Systems and Computers to Keep Costs Down
- Target Will Keep the Cost of Moving Merchandise Down
- Target Is a Good Neighbor
- Target Is a Growth Company
- Target Is Committed to Growth Within Its Markets and Region
- Target Is People[30]

" From that exercise, a comprehensive mission statement known as "Decision Guides" was developed, and distributed to employees, so they could follow for guidance. That mission statement came to be known as "Guides for Growth."

Thirteen executives signed off on the finished product, including McMillan and Kenneth Macke.[31] "Norman's work was so good, it became one of those documents read throughout the retail industry," said Pistner in *On Target: How the World's Hottest Retailer Hit a Bull's-Eye.* "In all my years in business, I don't remember a better document to guide a business by. People who worked at Target knew who they were when they read the document."[32]

Under the heading of "Running the Store/Target Is a Chain," the Guides for Growth specified that Target stores would "seek a high degree of uniformity in our operations." That translated to decision making applying to all stores, rather than decisions being made on an individual store basis.[33] In line with that desire to become more consistent across the board, Target introduced "Plannograms" in 1974.

Plannograms helped track in-stocks and merchandise presentation. Every nook and cranny of store space was accounted for and laid out accordingly.[34] Plannograms prevented stores from filling displays with other products when an item ran out, thereby maximizing shelf space, which made premium placement and the highest return.[35]

Guides for Growth affirmed Target's belief that young families ranked at the top of the customers they served. Countless examples illustrate how Target stayed true to that ideal. One of the more publicized occurred in May of 1977 when Target made the decision to pull *Penthouse, Playboy,* and similar magazines from its shelves, even though stocking the adult magazines made sense financially. Guides for Growth had a "Special Rule of Common Sense" pertaining to young families that stated: "A rule of common sense applies to certain specific areas of merchandise which significant numbers of our customers find offensive in a family store setting."[36]

According to Norman Macmillan, Target's vice president of planning at the time, "adult" magazine sales from the fifty-four existing Target stores were forecast to be $1 million in 1977, with at least $300,000 in profits. "We know it's a lot of money," McMillan said. "We figure we'll be giving up $120,000 in profit in one year on *Playboy* alone."[37]

The decision began with store managers, who initially opted to move the magazines to areas of the stores where kids could not see them. That led to placements behind the checkout counters in the hope of further limiting access. And, finally, the company ultimatum came: as of June 1, 1977, adult magazines were prohibited from being sold in Target stores.[38] "We're just trying to be consistent," McMillan explained. "We decided to take our stand. We have to declare what we want to stand for."[39]

The1974 earnings of Target—Dayton Hudson's low-margin group—moved back to 1971 levels before jumping 283 percent between 1974 and 1976.[40] From 1974 to 1975, sales went up 20 percent to $511.9 million, making the discounter Dayton Hudson Corporation's top chain in revenue.[41] In 1976, Target opened four new stores and sales rose to $600 million.

More Acquisitions

Target acquired Mervyn's in 1978. Based in Hayward, California, Mervyn's carried national brands of housewares, clothing, electronics, bedding, footwear, beauty products, and jewelry. Most Mervyn's stores were located in shopping malls, with the exception of a few that were free-standing.[42] The acquisition made Dayton Hudson the seventh-largest general merchandise retailer in the US. Target opened thirteen stores in 1979 and now had eighty stores in eleven states. Expansion continued with the opening of seventeen stores in 1980 and the acquisition of the Ayr-Way chain, a purchase that included forty stores and a distribution center in the Midwest. The stores were remodeled. The conversions were completed in November of 1981.[43] Ayr-Way's acquisition expanded Target's footprint eastward. Previously, the Milwaukee store had been the farthest east Target had reached. Ayr-Way, which opened in Indianapolis in 1961, had outlets in Kentucky, Illinois, and Ohio.[44] As profits continued to grow, Pistner and Macke were rewarded for their part in driving Target's recovery and success. Pistner was promoted to the newly created position of chairman of Target Stores and would move on to become Dayton Hudson president. Macke succeeded Pistner as Target president in 1976 and advanced to corporate president when Pistner left the company for Montgomery Ward & Co. early in 1981.

By the beginning of 1982, Target had expanded to 151 stores in seventeen Midwestern and southern States[45] and had sales of $2.1 billion.[46]

Target employed a strategy of using acquisitions to move into quality locations in new markets, which it followed in 1982 when it moved into California and Arizona by buying thirty-three Fedmart stores.[47] It purchased an additional fifty-one Gemco stores in California in 1986 and converted these to Target stores too.[48]

The move into California wasn't as smooth as Target had hoped, however. Stores occasionally ran out of merchandise, which wasn't the ideal first impression they wanted to create. But the experience would teach them to improve consumer research, along with the computer and satellite system it relied on to help with distribution and inventory control.[49]

"We have a long
heritage of community
involvement that includes
both financial support
and team member
volunteerism."

—BOB ULRICH, Target CEO

CHAPTER EIGHT

CHANGING OF THE GUARD

Kenneth Dayton retired from Dayton Hudson Corporation in June of 1983. It was the first time in the company's history that a Dayton family member was not involved. Not only was Kenneth remembered for being the last Dayton: he also was credited with playing a large part in forming the company's direction for moving forward. The Dayton brothers had long known that the day would come when the family ties to the company would no longer exist. Collectively, they had decided that the company would be fine if they left it without a Dayton on the board—they just needed to set into place a model of governance that would allow the Dayton Hudson Corporation to continue to grow and thrive.[1]

Dayton brothers Wally, Doug, and Don had served on the board until 1977. Meanwhile, brothers Ken and Bruce had continued as chair and CEO, affording the pair time to come up with a plan for who would manage and govern the company once the family had exited. Eventually, the responsibility fell to

Ken. He wanted to develop a governing system that would maximize the relationship between management and the board.[2]

The Achilles' Heel of the American Corporation

Ken Dayton felt that the board of directors was the "Achilles heel of the American Corporation."[3]

"Every time you find a business in trouble, you find a board of directors either unwilling or unable to fulfill its responsibilities," he wrote in a 1984 article for the *Harvard Business Review*. "The corollary of this conviction is that if we want to improve the performance of corporate America, then we must first improve the effectiveness of corporate boards of directors."[4]

In a 1986 speech Ken Dayton made to an Independent Sector Leadership/Management Forum, he revealed some of what he sought to create. "Governance is governance; it is not management. The board must be the primary force pressing the corporation for fulfillment of the obligations and the achievement of the potential of the corporation. Confusing the responsibilities of governance and management hampers the mission of the corporation.

"Again, governance is governance; management is management. The trick for management is to leave no voids, and the trick for the board is to see that management has a plan to fill any voids, *not* to leap in and fill them. If a board is managing the enterprise, the CEO is merely a figurehead, and the company is headed for trouble."[5]

Ken stressed his belief that, in order for the Dayton Hudson Corporation to run smoothly, there needed to be a division of labor between the board, the chair, and the CEO. Accordingly, he created criteria for the board of directors, the chair of the board, and the president and CEO. The criteria clearly defined the board's function, duties, and operations. As representative of the company's shareholders, the board needed to be the "primary force pressing the enterprise to the realization of its opportunities" and fulfilling its obligations to its customers, employees, and shareholders, as well as the communities in which the Dayton Hudson corporation operated.

The board therefore needed to "elect, monitor, appraise, advise, stimulate, support, reward, and if deemed necessary or desirable, change top management." In addition, the board would regularly discuss with the CEO matters that were of concern to him or her or to the board.[6]

> ❝ We developed a strong philosophy of management and governance and left the business with a heritage that exists . . . today. I think we maintained the highest ethical standards, which became a hallmark of that heritage.

Ken handed over updated timetables to the board's personnel committee, along with plans for the inevitable day when the company would no longer operate under family management. His diligence in creating the governance model delivered a map for guiding the company long after he and his brothers left the board. Kenneth wrote in July 2001: "We developed a strong philosophy of management and governance and left the business with a heritage that exists . . . today. I think we maintained the highest ethical standards, which became a hallmark of that heritage."[7]

The Five Percent Club

Ken Dayton made sure that the company's philanthropic position would be maintained going forward by leading the Minneapolis Chamber of Commerce to establish the Five Percent Club. Prior to the club's formation, the Dayton Corporation had given away 5 percent of its profits, which encouraged other companies to do the same and helped make philanthropy a part of the Twin Cities' culture. By 2007, the Five Percent Club—which had become the Keystone Club—had 214 members: 134 of those donated at the 5 percent level; the others donated 2 percent of their pretax profits.[8]

The Dayton brothers' commitment to philanthropy did not stop with corporate giving. Each brother also gave substantial amounts individually. For example, Kenneth Dayton's favorite cause was the Minnesota Orchestra. He and his wife, Judy, gave $2 million that went toward building Minneapolis's Orchestra Hall. And they gave a $15 million donation to the orchestra's endowment in 1994.[9]

The Dayton Hudson Foundation—as part of the change from Dayton Hudson Corporation to Target Corp.—was renamed the Target Foundation in 2000. It directed its efforts toward the Twin Cities' metro area; Target Corporate and Stores Organizational Giving focused on areas where Target operated offices and stores. Target's philanthropy also extended to humanitarian disaster relief, regardless of where the disaster occurred.

The policy directed funding to the following major areas:

■ Education, through signature programs such as Take Charge of Education and Target field trip grants.
■ The arts, by offering free access to major cultural institutions across the country.
■ Social services, including support for disaster preparedness, relief, and recovery.
■ Volunteerism; Target team members donate thousands of hours to community projects and partners nationwide, including Target House, which provides a home-away-from-home for families of children undergoing treatment at St. Jude Children's Research Hospital in Memphis.[10]

During the company's 2002 annual report, Bob Ulrich, Target CEO and chair of Target Corporation, spoke about the Daytons' influence on Target's giving. "Our guests . . . believe that the companies with whom they do business should embody unquestionable ethical standards and demonstrate a sincere commitment to the community. Target Corporation has embraced both of these values for many decades, in large part due to the leadership and legacy of the Dayton family. As a result of their vision . . . we have a long heritage of community involvement that includes both financial support and team member volunteerism. For nearly sixty years, we have contributed 5 percent of our federally taxable income to national and local non-profit programs that make our guests' communities safer and more attractive places to live and work."

Thwarting a Hostile Takeover

Dayton Hudson's maintained a distinct Minnesota flavor, even though the company had grown by leaps and bounds, and the Daytons no longer pulled the strings. In the process, the company earned a great deal of equity within the community. And the locals gave back in June of 1987 by aiding the company's cause when the Dart Group attempted a hostile takeover.[11]

Red flags went up when company executives noticed that 30 percent of Dayton Hudson stock (approximately thirty million shares) had been traded. Clearly, something was amiss.

Ken Macke, who had risen to CEO, and other Dayton Hudson executives did not want the Dart Group to pull off the takeover. Macke sought help from the state of Minnesota.

Many citizens and various charities lobbied on Dayton Hudson's behalf. Minnesota governor Rudy Perpich called a special session of the state legislature to examine Minnesota's takeover statute. Dayton Hudson presented its case to the legislature, reminding them of the company's many contributions to Minnesota, which included donations, providing jobs, and stimulating the local economy, to name a few. They cautioned that a Dart Group takeover would result in the breakup of Dayton Hudson Corporation, which would hurt the community.

Dayton Hudson's case did not fall on deaf ears; the Dart Group had a history. The Haft family controlled the Dart Group and had been involved in previous attempts at hostile takeovers, which brought financial gains to the Dart Group, but otherwise delivered devasting consequences.[12] For example, in 1986, the Dart Group attempted a hostile takeover of Safeway, and made a $97 million profit on its shares. Although Safeway successfully avoided the takeover, in the aftermath, their debt forced the company to close 331 stores and lay off over 8,600 employees.[13]

Minnesota acted in a favorable direction for Dayton Hudson Corporation—the state's solid-gold corporate citizen. Laws were enacted designed to protect Dayton Hudson and other Minnesota companies from hostile takeovers.[14]

"You have to be new and fresh, always doing something interruptive. Retailing has to be noticed."

—JOHN PELLEGRENE,
Target Marketing Guru

CHAPTER NINE

BOB ULRICH, AN EXCEPTIONAL LEADER

B ob Ulrich had recently graduated from the University of Minnesota with a degree in speech and journalism when he began his career at Dayton's as a merchandise trainee in 1967. If anybody ever validated the Dayton brothers' intentions to hire talented people and groom them for executive greatness, Ulrich would be the guy. Detail oriented and extremely private, Ulrich acquired a reputation as a talented merchandiser while advancing up the corporate ladder.

In January of 1981, he was named Dayton's vice president for merchandise, sales promotion, and presentation, and by December of that same year he became president and CEO of Diamond's department store, a division of Dayton Hudson Corporation. In 1984, Ulrich was promoted to president of Target Stores, and he'd advanced to chairman and CEO of Target by 1987, at which time the chain had grown to 247 stores in twenty-two states and had reported revenues of $4.3 billion the year prior.[1]

" In 1984, Ulrich was promoted to president
of Target Stores, and he'd advanced
to chairman and CEO of Target by 1987,
at which time the chain had grown to
247 stores in twenty-two states and had
reported revenues of $4.3 billion the
year prior.

Ulrich's detail-oriented persona and slant toward innovation played well during Target's strategic move into the Southeast in 1989. The thirty stores that opened there gave the chain a coast-to-coast footprint and introduced the P-88 (P for Prototype) design. P-88 differed from the layout of the earlier model, P-86. Among the changes were wider aisles in the more popular sections, and side-to-side aisles, rather than front-to-back aisles, were put into place in major aisles. Additionally, the ceilings over perimeter shopping sections were raised. The P-88 design attempted to convey a feeling of spaciousness.[2]

Target also opted to test a new pricing strategy. An every-day-low-pricing strategy was introduced that cut sales promotions and brought prices to consistently low levels. By negotiating bargains on the purchases of its newer products, Target was able to remain competitive while dropping prices.

In addition to the new store designs and pricing strategy—along with the innovations triggered by the chain's initial California efforts—Target brought along its time-tested formula of clean stores, trend-conscious clothes, and a stress-free return policy. Target also adjusted merchandising to better serve customers in the Southeast. For example, some of the stores sold fishing tackle that included saltwater gear or stocked products for recreational water use year-round.[3]

Target's expanded presence in California and the Southeast gave the chain 407 stores in thirty-two states and helped drive sales to $7.52 billion in 1989, which amounted to a profit of $449 million and accounted for more than half of parent company Dayton Hudson's operating profits.[4]

Sometimes You Just Need a Bigger Target

Target introduced the 169,000-square-foot Greatland store in 1990, opening at Southport Centre in Apple Valley, Minnesota, a Twin Cities suburb.[5]

> Target introduced the 169,000-square-foot Greatland store in 1990, opening at Southport Centre in Apple Valley, Minnesota, a Twin Cities suburb.

The average Target store was 110,000 square feet. The Greatland concept featured larger departments, wider aisles, and newer features like one-hour photo developing. Other enhancements not seen in a typical Target included electronic scanners, which were located around the store and allowed customers to check prices; sit-down eating space for over a hundred people; color-coded sections; and thirty-two checkout lanes. Normal Targets had just sixteen to eighteen.[6]

In 1990, Dayton Hudson Corporation bought Marshall Field's. Many questioned their wisdom, given the climate—grand, upscale department stores had seemingly seen better days. Would absorbing Marshall Field's hamstring Target, Dayton Hudson's star? Hardly.

Ulrich examined Target and realized the chain's price points had gone up, which hurt competitiveness. Acting on those findings, he deemphasized hardlines—items like hardware, lawn equipment, automotive, electronics, sporting goods, health and beauty products, and toys—and moved to emphasize soft goods, such as apparel, linens, and footwear.[7]

Stan Pohmer, a senior buyer at Target from 1983 to 1996, said Target "really started getting focused" under Ulrich. "Besides being a good merchandiser, Bob took the time to really understand the total business. He understood you couldn't be all things to all people."[8] Ulrich set high expectations for managers, instituting quantitative measurables and detailed job reviews.[9]

By 1993, Target had revenues of $11.7 billion with operating profits of $662 million. Ulrich's competitive side was on full display during a 1993 episode when Walmart got under his skin. Their ads claimed that their prices were lower than Target's. Returning fire, Target ran ads criticizing Walmart for using incorrect price comparisons, adding: "This would never have happened if Sam Walton was alive."[10] Walmart dropped their ad; Ulrich claimed victory.

Ulrich Moves Up

Mervyn's continued to perform poorly, as did Dayton Hudson's full-line department stores, which led to Ken Macke stepping down as Dayton Hudson's CEO early in 1994.[11]

Ulrich succeeded him. Some believed he'd staged a coup and took over the position. Sally Apgar of the *Star Tribune* wrote the following: "There is wide speculation in business circles that Ulrich and his lieutenants had a hand in persuading key members of the board to ask Macke to retire as chairman and chief executive officer in April 1994."[12]

Ulrich believed in gathering the critical data, taking risks, and moving on quickly from failure.[13] He also preached a "Targetization" of Dayton Hudson, which the *Star Tribune* later defined as "a cultural revolution in which many people and business practices from Target have been transplanted to other divisions."[14]

Under Macke, the company had streamlined from over a dozen businesses to three divisions: the department stores—Dayton's, Hudson's, and Marshall Field's; Mervyn's; and Target. Macke also had cut expenses and repositioned Mervyn's—a move that had not found success. Ulrich set out to further streamline the company and save money wherever he thought was necessary. Speed and efficiency were the backbone of his business philosophy. At his first annual meeting after becoming CEO, he told investors, "Speed is Life."[15] He was a great admirer of General Electric's chairman Jack Welch.

> Ulrich set out to further streamline the company and save money wherever he thought was necessary. Speed and efficiency were the backbone of his business philosophy. At his first annual meeting after becoming CEO, he told investors, "Speed is Life."

The month prior to Ulrich's speech to stockholders, Welch had spoken to the Economic Club of Detroit, and told the group: "Boundaryless behavior evaluates ideas on their merit, not on the rank of the person who came up with them. . . . Boundaryless behavior laughs at little kingdoms called finance, engineering, manufacturing and marketing sending each other specs and memos and instead gets them all together in the same room to wrestle with issues as a team."[16]

Ulrich issued a memo to lower-rank employees that expressed a desire to create this same "boundaryless organization" and noted that if Dayton Hudson wanted to be a "truly world-class structure we need to aggressively break down any barriers among divisions, and to create an organization without boundaries."

Ulrich expressed his wishes for those employees to embrace the concept and help in any way they could. The memo also said, "Be prepared in the coming months to break out of the 'old' way of thinking and be open to the 'new' way of sharing, interacting and overcoming the barriers among our corporate divisions."[17]

Ulrich sought to break down the "artificial barriers and sibling rivalries between the three operating divisions," bringing forth a "delayering process" that saw layoffs made to create a leaner operation that could make quicker decisions. Duplicated positions within the divisions were also eliminated to consolidate functions wherever possible and make the company more efficient.[18] Despite holding the company's top position, Ulrich held true to his reclusive nature. He never spoke to the media. He even was known to reserve comment from the company's investors. At Target's 2003 annual meeting, Ulrich irritated investors by not fielding questions at the end of the meeting, an uncommon move for a CEO.[19]

Two Unique Offerings

Target introduced two unique offerings in 1995: SuperTarget stores, and a Target Store credit card. The first SuperTarget launched in Omaha, Nebraska, in March of 1995, bringing to life a 190,000-square-foot store featuring sixty-five checkout lanes. The offering delivered the ultimate one-stop shopping experience, including a grocery section stocked with Target's newly introduced Archer Farms—the chain's first grocery-owned brand—which brought an exclusive line of premium grocery products including staples such as bread, milk, pasta, and bottled water. A second SuperTarget opened in Lawrence, Kansas, later on that year.

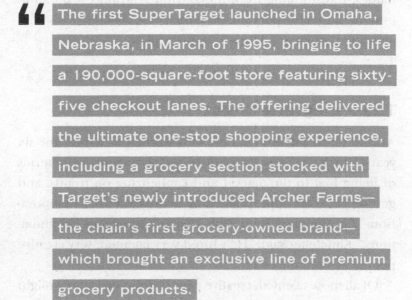

The first SuperTarget launched in Omaha, Nebraska, in March of 1995, bringing to life a 190,000-square-foot store featuring sixty-five checkout lanes. The offering delivered the ultimate one-stop shopping experience, including a grocery section stocked with Target's newly introduced Archer Farms—the chain's first grocery-owned brand—which brought an exclusive line of premium grocery products.

Target's first credit card was known as the "Target Guest Card," making Target the first mass merchant to offer a private-label card. By September 2001, twenty million consumers had the card.[20]

Ulrich introduced a three-year program in 1996 that had the auspicious goal of cutting $200 million from operating expenses by mid-1998.[21] Folded within that program was Dayton Hudson's 1997 announcement that it would sell or close thirty-five Mervyn's stores, twenty-five of which were in Georgia and Florida. Widespread speculation suggested that the remaining 275 stores, which were spread across fourteen states, would also be sold.[22]

Target continued to lead the way for Dayton Hudson Corporation. In light of its performance, the corporation changed names, transforming from the Dayton Hudson Corporation into the Target Corporation on January 13, 2000. Ulrich's "Targetization" of Dayton Hudson was complete.

The Pellegrene Effect

According to Jeff Klinefelter, who worked at Target for six years, Ulrich was "very competitive and very aggressive in terms of being first to the market and capitalizing on trends, and getting out at the appropriate time to drive the cycle of innovation." "At the same time, Bob Ulrich appreciates his limitations," Klinefelter said. "He's hired very talented, very creative people to fill in the blanks."[23]

Of all those talented, creative people, John Pellegrene might have been the best. The marketing guru is generally credited for leading Target's never-ending mission to set itself apart from competitors as an upscale discounter. Pellegrene moved to Target in 1988 after serving as the senior vice president of marketing at Dayton's and Hudson's department stores. He'd more than distinguished himself with the 1985 introduction of Santabear, a stuffed bear that became an immediate Christmas icon. Dayton's and Hudson's supply of four hundred thousand bears sold out before Thanksgiving that first year.[24] Approximately 120 Santabear products were brought to market, including children's pajamas and ice cream makers. The lovable bear became a part of Christmas, and a new Santabear was introduced every year through 2007.

According to Jan Apple, an advertising and marketing consultant, Pellegrene was "incredibly creative and doesn't see the world the way other people do." "He sees the big picture. . . . He doesn't have to start at the beginning to get to the end. . . . You see him getting impatient if you go on and on about the details," Apple said.[25]

Rod Eaton, who worked in Dayton Hudson's graphics production workshop, described Pellegrene as someone who "thinks at the speed of light. . . . A lot of times you feel he's got a hundred other things on his mind."[26]

According to Pellegrene: "You have to be new and fresh, always doing something interruptive. Retailing has to be noticed." Pellegrene sifted through many ideas from many sources to find the ones he liked. "The concept is to run 1,000 [ideas] by you and cherry pick 10," Pellegrene said.[27]

Pellegrene didn't have an ego, and he readily shared credit for his ideas. He allowed that theater designers in the Twin Cities had a strong influence on Santabear's creation. "When you serve on boards of art institutions, they think you're giving something," Pellegrene said. "But the ideas come back to Dayton's."[28]

Once Pellegrene assumed the top marketing responsibilities for Target Stores, he effectively directed his creativity toward the chain. During Target's 1989 move into the Southeast, Pellegrene's efforts fueled the launch. He enlisted Wynonna and Naomi Judd—who hailed from Kentucky—in a TV commercial that featured the mother-daughter singing team performing an altered version of "Shop Around." The ad ran nationally, but clearly targeted the Southeast. Ulrich, who kept a low profile, said of the campaign: "As you go into new markets, you need something to capture people's attention."[29]

Another significant marketing effort came in 1990 when Target reached an agreement to pay the NBA's Minnesota Timberwolves $250,000 a year to name the team's new arena the "Target Center." The deal, which had Pellegrene's fingerprints all over it, included Target sponsorship of TV and radio broadcasts, player appearances at Target stores, and Target signage featuring the red bullseye inside and outside of the arena. The arrangement cast Target as a front-runner in the arena of corporate sponsorships for professional sports teams.[30]

The Target Center became the third US pro sports facility to bear the name of a corporate sponsor. ARCO Arena, home of the NBA's Sacramento Kings, and the Great Western Forum, home of the Los Angeles Lakers, were the other two. Kemper Arena, which had been the home of the Kings before they relocated from Kansas City to Sacramento, and the Carrier Dome— home of Syracuse University's football, men's basketball, and lacrosse teams—had commercial names; however, these sponsors were involved in the construction of those facilities.[31]

Santabear's continued success led to the introduction of another Christmas character in 1997, "Snowden the Snowman"—a toy created by and sold exclusively at Target. Pellegrene didn't wait until Christmas to get people acquainted with Snowden, either, and introduced the new character at the "Christmas in July" celebration in New York City. Snowden danced with the famed Rockettes while twenty other Snowden characters worked the street corners of Manhattan, handing out ten thousand bottles of Snowden water. Target priced Snowden at $15. Snowden boutiques were created in every Target store, and the character's image adorned countless items, such as sweatshirts, cookie jars, and baby bibs. For the first time, Target dedicated an entire section of the store to one promotion—The Snowden Shop. The shop featured a variety of Snowden-themed merchandise from fleece blankets to gift wrap. Snowden was also used on in-store signage and Food Avenue tray liners.[32]

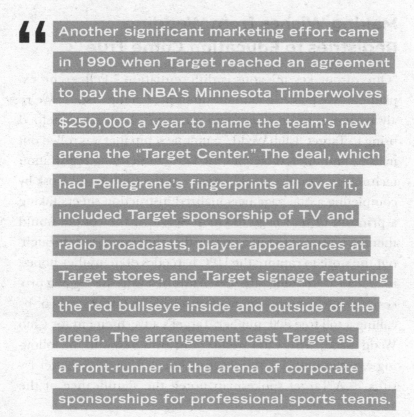

" Another significant marketing effort came in 1990 when Target reached an agreement to pay the NBA's Minnesota Timberwolves $250,000 a year to name the team's new arena the "Target Center." The deal, which had Pellegrene's fingerprints all over it, included Target sponsorship of TV and radio broadcasts, player appearances at Target stores, and Target signage featuring the red bullseye inside and outside of the arena. The arrangement cast Target as a front-runner in the arena of corporate sponsorships for professional sports teams.

The year before Snowden's introduction, Target sponsored a White House appearance by the singer LeAnn Rimes during the national tree-lighting ceremony. The following year, Rimes was not a part of the celebration when Target sent eight dancing Snowdens to the event instead. Snowden also appeared in the Hollywood Christmas parade and made guest appearances on the TV shows *Chicago Hope* and *Suddenly Susan*.[33] Snowden was also brought to life in a book by the same name, written by Nancy Carlson. Snowden's marketing in July of 1997 also included county fairs and the NBC *Today* show.[34]

Making Wishes from Wedding Registries to Education Come True

"One of our key missions is differentiation," Pellegrene explained. "We make an extreme attempt at being first. . . . We're always trying to do something unique."[35] Pellegrene helped bring to Target "Club Wedd," a unique setup that was rolled out in 1995 and offered couples the latest in wedding registration technology. Couples would register at the Club Wedd kiosk by completing a one-page personalized instruction sheet. Taking a printout of that page to Guest Services, the couple would then be given a barcode scanner that they could use throughout the store to capture the UPC barcodes of items they hoped to receive as wedding gifts. Once finished with the tagging process, their selections were made available at Target stores or by calling a toll-free 800 number. Target's advertisement for Club Wedd asked, "Why Club Wedd?" and answered with the following explanation: "It's as easy as making a wish. With better results."[36] A Target spokesman noted the significance of the registry. "People have been pulling bridal registry lists from department stores and shopping at Target for years. Now Target can offer them the convenience of our own registry."[37] More than 125,000 couples registered at Club Wedd that first year.[38]

Pellegrene is also credited with helping to create "Take Charge of Education," a charitable initiative launched in 1997 to aid schools. When customers shopped at Target using their Target Guest Card, a portion of the purchase would go back to the school of their choice. The program also nudged customers to get Target debit and credit cards. By the time it ended in 2015, the program had distributed in excess of $432 million to more than one hundred thousand schools in the United States.[39]

Target introduced an unnamed dog in a 1999 TV spot during the incredibly successful marketing campaign "Sign of the Times," which featured the bullseye trademark in various unexpected places, including the face of a white bull terrier. The English Bull Terrier, who had Target's bullseye logo painted around its left eye, became a contemporary icon,[40] appearing in TV commercials, on the Target website, and throughout its stores. Bullseye earned the distinction of becoming only the second dog to have its wax likeness put on display in Madame Tussaud's Wax Museum.[41]

Target and Target's marketing arm—which Pellegrene was a huge part of—operated differently from most department stores, which didn't include marketing on product decisions until late in the process, and then only to advertise merchandise. Pellegrene noted the difference. "We don't look at advertising as purely paper and film. We are a dimensional advertising department. We are not a department that simply deals in conventional media. We deal in marketing programs that will also bring millions of dollars into the company in perpetuity."[42]

> **"** Target introduced an unnamed dog in a 1999 TV spot during the incredibly successful marketing campaign "Sign of the Times," which featured the bullseye trademark in various unexpected places, including the face of a white bull terrier. The English Bull Terrier, who had Target's bullseye logo painted around its left eye, became a contemporary icon, appearing in TV commercials, on the Target website, and throughout its stores. Bullseye earned the distinction of becoming only the second dog to have its wax likeness put on display in Madame Tussaud's Wax Museum.

Narrowing Target's focus to promoting only the brand, Target Corp. sold Marshall Field's (which included Dayton's and Hudson's department stores; both had been renamed Marshall Field's in 2001) to May Department Stores Corp. for $3.2 billion in 2004. The corporation also sold its Mervyn's department stores to an investment consortium for approximately $1.65 billion. Mervyn's credit-card receivables were sold to GE Consumer Finance for $475 million.[43]

When Ulrich retired in 2008, Target ranked as the No. 2 discount retailer in the United States, with $59 billion in sales, more than 366,000 employees, and 1,613 stores. During Ulrich's reign as CEO, Target's sales quadrupled, and net earnings increased ninefold.[44]

"Our idea is that you can have a beautiful design and good quality, and don't have to spend a million for it. The trick is that price has to be right."

—JOHN PELLEGRENE,
Target Marketing Guru

CHAPTER TEN

MICHAEL GRAVES AND BEYOND

Michael Graves's postmodern architecture first splashed onto the scene with his design for the municipal center in Portland, Oregon. Other notable Graves designs included Walt Disney World's Dolphin and Swan Hotels, and the Spanish Mission–inspired library in San Juan Capistrano, California. When Target backed the Washington Monument project as a corporate sponsor in 1997, they hired Graves to design a translucent sheath to cover the scaffolding that surrounded the monument during the restoration. Graves's work hid what had been viewed as an eyesore.[1]

Target's relationship with Graves laid the foundation for what would become a major income stream. He signed a deal to create a line of private-label products that were launched in 1999. All Target stores were fitted with a Michael Graves boutique to display his workable home furnishings. The introduction of Graves's product line included a national advertising campaign, a showcase home featuring Graves's designs at the

Minneapolis Parade of Homes Spring Preview event, and a launch at New York's Whitney Museum of American Art in January of 1999.

"They asked me to lunch," Graves told the *New York Times* in 2011, "and said, 'We've been knocking you off for 20 years,' and said, 'Maybe you'd like to come and try designing for us, if we can keep the price at a Target range.'"[2]

Ron Johnson, vice president and general manager for home decor at Target, said of Graves: "We didn't hire him because of his celebrity status. We don't think we really need to sell Michael as much as we need to sell good design."[3]

The Michael Graves Design Collection included items such as tea kettles, picture frames, clocks, cutlery, wine racks, hand mixers, rose vases, toasters, utensils, garden furniture, and other products. The line of approximately 150 products ranged in price from a $3.99 spatula to a $499 patio table and chair set.[4] Graves's designs were fun. The spatula he spoke of had a bulbous Wedgewood-blue handle. In addition to looking good, his products were also designed to work well. "We used colors that are somber and shapes that are anthropomorphic," Graves said. "But you know which end to pick up."[5]

Once one of his designs had been conceived, it would take six months to a year to bring the product to life. Target would "typically" make a first order of eighty thousand units. If the product moved, a reorder would occur. Continued demand might lead to a decision to stock that product for several years.[6] "Occasionally, something will last for a few years, like our toaster," Graves said. "Our toilet bowl brush outsold any product at Target." However, save for rare exceptions, once a Graves product ceased to be on the shelves, it would not return.[7]

Target and Graves enjoyed a thirteen-year relationship that brought to fruition designs for over two thousand products.

"Some modernist designers make utensils so you wouldn't know which end to pick up," Graves said. "In our case we try to be very clear about where you put your hand, which end you use to turn the eggs over. The color [becomes] a metaphor for use. A blue handle might signal that it's cool. The red whistle on a Target teakettle we hope indicates in some subtle way that it's hot."[8] That relationship had originated in marketing, and moved to merchandising, further displaying Target's ability to look outside the box for new ways to do things.

 Target and Graves enjoyed a thirteen-year relationship that brought to fruition designs for over two thousand products.

Paving the Way

Not only did Graves's exclusive product line produce revenue for Target, it paved the way to bring on board additional private-label products. Others included new lines by fashion designers Philippe Starck, Mossimo Giannulli, and Steven Sprouse; makeup artist Sonia Kashuk; and designer Todd Oldham. These private labels enhanced Target's fashion edge and generated revenues while providing the private labels with direct-to-retail licensing, thereby avoiding traditional complications such as markdowns, capital intensive inventory, and global production.[9]

These partnerships helped spark a dramatic shift in how fashion was perceived. In the past, in order to buy unique fashion items by edgy, hip designers, customers had to go to top-of-the-line department stores—which obviously carried some snob appeal for the customers and the designers. Given Target's ability to offer unique items created by trendy designers, consumers did not view shopping at Target as lowbrow. That consumer behavior directed upscale vendors to reconsider where they wanted to sell their wares. Target became a desirable destination based on the sheer number of shoppers that frequented the chain in comparison to the dwindling numbers at department stores. Vendors began to contact Target hoping to find placement inside their stores.

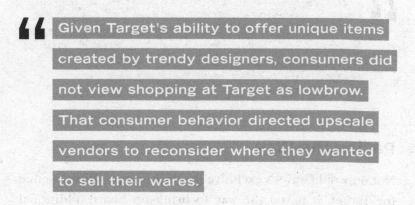

> Given Target's ability to offer unique items created by trendy designers, consumers did not view shopping at Target as lowbrow. That consumer behavior directed upscale vendors to reconsider where they wanted to sell their wares.

The Pros of Proprietary

These private-label products bolstered Target's differentiation strategy.[10] Introducing proprietary products cut a clear path toward raising profit margins. A good product made in house could be better controlled, thereby allowing for better pricing because Target could now dodge the marketing costs and markups that become necessary when stocking a manufacturer's brand. Target's exclusivity to its private-label product lines eliminated price competition for the product. This control allowed Target not only to offer unique products, but also to implement a healthy markup without running off customers in the process.[11]

The designer partnerships also reaffirmed the "Tar-zhay" moniker and Target's reputation for "cheap chic." "Our idea is that you can have a beautiful design and good quality, and don't have to spend a million for it," John Pellegrene said. "The trick is that price has to be right, no matter how beautiful it is."[12]

After all, Target's slogan was "Expect More. Pay Less."—a slogan established "to reflect the unique retail experience offered at Target." The promise served as an expression of Target's "commitment to community giving and offering guests value, quality and service, all in a fun and inviting store environment."[13]

"We didn't live up to that responsibility."

—GREGG STEINHAFEL,
Target CEO on Target's security breach

CHAPTER ELEVEN

OH, CANADA, AND GETTING HACKED

Speculation about Target expanding into Canada began to circulate in the aftermath of the 2004 sales of Marshall Field's and Mervyn's. The $5.3 billion boost gave Target Corporation an excess of cash. It was easy to see that Target could make a strategic move by acquiring Zellers, a Canadian discount chain. Such a move would expedite the company's entrance into Canada.[1] However, Target did not head north of the border at that point, even though Canada appeared to be an ideal landscape for Target to operate in.

The financial climate played a role in the decision. By 2008, deregulation had thrust the United States into a financial crisis, bringing about the worst economic disaster since the Great Depression. Few were immune from the effects of that recession, including Target.

Still, a Canadian invasion continued to percolate until 2011 when Target began negotiating with Hudson's Bay Co., to purchase 220 Zellers leases. Hudson's Bay had bought Zellers in

1978, and the Canadian discount chain performed well until
Walmart moved into Canada in 1994. Walmart's success cost
Zellers market share, and eventually forced the chain's management to recognize that its leases had more value than its
operations. That prompted a desire to sell the leases and made
Target the ideal suitor, particularly given Target's desire to enter Canada and experience rapid growth.

Zellers' management alerted Target to their intention to sell
its leases. They also made it known that Walmart had interest.
Even though Walmart eventually withdrew, Target still paid
1.85 billion Canadian dollars to purchase the 220 Zellers leases
from Hudson's Bay Co. At the time, Target operated 1,752
stores, all within the United States.

After spending an average of $10 million to $11 million per
location to convert each Zellers, Target opened fifty stores during the first half of 2013, its first year in Canada.[2] The early re-
turns were not encouraging.

A month before Target's first Canadian stores opened in
March, the company held a meeting of senior-level employees
in Mississauga, Ontario. The goal of the meeting was to evaluate whether Target was ready to open its doors on schedule. At
risk was the first impression Target would make on Canadian
customers.

A Distribution Disaster

Several problems were discussed—including supply chain. Getting a distribution system up to speed so that it was ready to
stock 124 stores had been a huge task, particularly within Target's self-imposed two-year time frame for doing so. Tasks that
had to be done included customizing and remodeling stores,

hiring and training staff, building and stocking distribution centers, deciding on an IT supply chain management system—then implementing that system, and stocking the actual stores with product.[3] Moving products from distribution centers to store shelves had not gone smoothly, which created the prospect of stores with empty shelves; meanwhile, transactions weren't being processed well due to a flawed checkout system, and the inventory systems weren't functioning properly due to new technology that few understood. In hindsight, the individuals running the Canada operation should have asked for more time. However, such a pause would have caused numerous delays in planned store openings. So Target surged on, opening on schedule.

By the fall of 2013, most of the scheduled 124 stores had opened. Clearly, the earlier problems that senior-level employees had identified had lingered. Other problems arose. Of all those problems, supply chain might have been the worst.

Target's US operation had supply chain technology tailor-made for its needs, and had honed it for years. But it didn't translate into operating in a foreign country. Had Target wanted to use that technology in Canada, major tweaking would have been necessary to handle new needs. Prominent among them was the need to adapt to Canadian currency—an adjustment that would have required a lot of time. Rather than adjusting their existing technology, Target elected to use a different technology in Canada.

And they brought in an outside supplier to build a new system. SAP became their system of choice for Canada. Able to store vast amounts of data about every store product, SAP was equipped to forecast product demand and replenish stocks, while also managing distribution centers. Because the SAP system was more sophisticated than what Target used in the

United States, Target eventually planned to convert their US system to SAP as well. Such a move would have aligned stores in both countries.[4] Though SAP brought advanced technology, implementing the system came with a steep learning curve. Target couldn't avoid a mess, even though they hired a company to consult on SAP.

Target stocked approximately 75,000 products and each required a dossier of information that needed to be properly registered in the system. Had Target expanded its US system to include Canada, those products would have already been logged. Instead, all of the data had to be reentered. This was an inherently exhaustive process, and many errors were made.

> " Target stocked approximately 75,000 products and each required a dossier of information that needed to be properly registered in the system. Had Target expanded its US system to include Canada, those products would have already been logged. Instead, all of the data had to be reentered. This was an inherently exhaustive process, and many errors were made.

Due to the litany of problems stemming from the technology systems, the company wasn't able to properly order products from vendors. This led to problems with processing goods through warehouses, which ultimately led to an inability to properly stock store shelves in an efficient manner—often leaving stores with empty shelves. Or stores would have too much of one product and not enough of another.

The nightmare festered at the three large distribution centers Target had built to serve its Canadian stores. Charles O'Shea, vice president and senior analyst at Moody's Investor's Service, observed in a 2014 article in the *Windsor Star* that, "One of the key factors behind Walmart's success over the past 40 years has been just that it has always had the ability to build about a year's worth of stores without having to add any distribution capability. That is Target's US model, and the company deviated from that model to get into Canada."[5]

Fluidity and harmony are needed to successfully run a retail distribution center. Like a basketball center playing the high post, the goal is to take the pass then dish off the ball to another player. In Target's case, the distribution centers were intended to receive the goods from countless vendors everywhere, briefly hold those goods, then quickly load them into trucks and ship them to waiting stores. Instead, Target's distribution centers swelled with product, far exceeding what could possibly be sold—even if the centers managed to find a way to get that product stocked in stores. The culprit? Crazy projections. Target lacked the historical data to make accurate forecasts about buying patterns in Canada, and thus had no idea how much product it needed to order from vendors.[6]

The overly optimistic sales forecasts were derived from Target's US operations, where the Target brand was strong and forecasts had cause to be positive. Forecasts reflecting the hope of successfully establishing a market in a new country would have been more accurate.

The replenishment system brought another set of problems. In a perfect retail world, items that sell quickly are replaced by new stock on the shelves thanks to an educated replenishment system that alerts distribution centers to send along the new stock. Target's low-level analysts were responsible for forecasting the right numbers. Thus, they could be blamed for mistakes. Eventually, the analysts discovered a way to turn off the replenishment system's automatic mechanism for reordering, which allowed them to avoid blame, but left the operation vulnerable due to incorrect replenishment reports.[7]

Vendors shared responsibility for the over-ordering too. They figured that if Zellers—a run-down discount chain—had managed to do a certain amount of business, Target would logically need far more product.[8]

Point-of-sale systems presented another problem. Transactions were not processed properly due in part to cash terminals freezing and prolonged periods of inactivity while the terminals booted for operation. Incorrect change was often dispensed at self-checkout locations.

Location, Location, Location

The locations of Target's Canadian stores didn't help their cause, either. Opening in locales where Zellers had once operated had looked brilliant on paper: Target would have an instant footprint in Canada at locations where existing stores could be remodeled. But unfortunately for Target, many of the stores were located in areas that were not populated by the typical customer Target sought and loved—middle-class and with a sense of style—and they did not provide good shells for conversions. Many Zellers were located in shopping malls, making them less accessible than a freestanding outlet. Even though Target had repurposed the Zellers stores—which consumers perceived as being grades below Target's high-quality reputation—the new Targets (save for the familiar red and white trim) had remained Zellers in the minds of their guests.

Simply stated, Target's Canadian stores were not able to create the same buzz that shoppers in the United States felt. Expecting more and paying less wasn't happening. So long as Target wasn't able to fulfill the promise of providing high-quality, fun, and trendy merchandise, it was your everyday discount store north of the border. Canadian Target stores were not Tar-zhay.[9]

> So long as Target wasn't able to fulfill the promise of providing high-quality, fun, and trendy merchandise, it was your everyday discount store north of the border. Canadian Target stores were not Tar-zhay.

If Target wasn't giving shoppers a special experience, why not simply shop for items at lower prices? Shopping for lower prices directed customers to Walmart, which had been in Canada since 1994. Walmart had always been the top dog for low prices, so they were more than happy to compete with Target in a price war, a competition Target wasn't equipped to win.

Target's home sections and apparel had shown promising results. Nondiscretionary items like health-care products and food did not. Consumers thought that Target's prices for those items were higher than competitors', and that contributed to the lull.[10]

"The big problem that Target had was that it was not competitive with Walmart, it was not competitive with Canadian Tire and it was not competitive with Costco to a certain extent," said David Soberman, a marketing professor at the University of Toronto, in a 2015 article in the *Star Tribune*. "Canadian Tire and Walmart are really tough competitors, and if you make basic mistakes that business school tells you not to make, it will be really tough."[11]

Canadian Target: Not a US Target Experience

Higher prices along with the fact that some brands and products—Cherry Coke, for instance—were unavailable added to Target's negative perception, particularly among customers who had visited US Target stores, where they had enjoyed an altogether different experience.[12]

Target's ambitious plan of opening an entire nation of stores—literally overnight—had not been a prudent move. If they had progressed incrementally, they could have encountered problems on a small scale, fixed them, and moved on. Instead, when they experienced problems—as they did with their supply chain—they experienced them on a grand scale.

According to a Forum Research poll done for the *Toronto Globe and Mail*, just 18 percent of Target customers surveyed were "very satisfied" with Target stores in May of 2014, down from 32 percent the previous May.[13] Target's Canadian effort lost $941 million before taxes in its first year, 2013. By midsummer of 2014, Target acknowledged its many blunders by offering a mea culpa to its Canadian shoppers via a YouTube video.

Damien Liddle, Target Canada's senior corporate counsel, said on the clip: "Maybe we didn't put our best foot forward when we entered into Canada. We had some disappointments when we opened. Certainly, we think we disappointed our guests. But here at headquarters and at our store teams we're working really hard to give everybody that unique Target experience."[14]

Hopes to salvage Canada's operation ran high, but most wondered if it had been damaged beyond repair.

A Security Breach

If the news in Canada wasn't bad enough already, Target took another crushing blow when a security breach occurred at the end of 2013. Hackers compromised the software in Target stores, stealing credit and debit card information from their customers.

On January 10, 2014, Target announced that another seventy million customers had been exposed to the data breach, and that customers' email addresses had also been compromised. This further stoked fear among consumers, who worried that they had been exposed to fraudulent charges—meanwhile, the court of public opinion indicted Target for dragging its feet when it came to warning customers about what had happened.

Target's response came four days later, on January 14. Gregg Steinhafel, who had succeeded Bob Ulrich as Target's chairman, president, and chief executive officer, released a letter in which he stressed that Target's top priority was taking care of its guests and helping them feel confident about shopping at Target—that it was Target's responsibility to protect their information. He allowed, "We didn't live up to that responsibility," and followed with, "I am truly sorry."

Not since a 2007 cyberattack on T.J. Maxx had a major US retailer suffered a breach on the scale of Target's. The Target cyberattack proved to be a precursor for other security breaches that would involve Home Depot, JP Morgan, and the US Postal Service.[15]

> On January 10, 2014, Target announced that another seventy million customers had been exposed to the data breach, and that customers' email addresses had also been compromised. This further stoked fear among consumers, who worried that they had been exposed to fraudulent charges— meanwhile, the court of public opinion indicted Target for dragging its feet when it came to warning customers about what had happened.

Despite sagging sales in the United States and Canada, Target made a sizable effort to regain the faith of its customers by spending $100 million to improve security standards, including the implementation of chip-and-PIN technology for debit and credit cards.[16]

Steinhafel's Impact

Steinhafel had begun his career at Target in 1979. Target had launched several impressive growth initiatives while he led the company. Among them had been the creation of the CityTarget store, which had an urban feel in comparison to Target's signature locations. These smaller stores were opened in downtown locations in 2012, giving the chain an inroad to a different arena. TargetExpress had also been introduced, creating a small-format store designed to compete against drugstores, dollar stores, and Walmart. And then the PFresh format came to fruition, offering customers a limited assortment of groceries and fresh food.

However, Target had also grown somewhat stale on Steinhafel's watch. Stores had expanded their food offerings, ostensibly to attract more shoppers, who would arrive to pick up a dozen eggs and then venture into the other parts of the store to make a higher-priced purchase, like a pair of designer jeans. But that strategy wasn't working.

Designer lines had lost their luster, effectively removing the chain's chic factor—and the security breach and the failure in Canada sealed Steinhafel's fate. He resigned on May 5, 2014. CFO John Mulligan stepped in as the interim replacement for the veteran Target executive of thirty-five years.

Following Steinhafel's resignation, Target's board released a statement that praised him by saying, "He held himself personally accountable and pledged that Target would emerge a better company. We are grateful to him for his tireless leadership and will always consider him a member of the Target family."[17]

Clearly, the board had wanted Steinhafel out, even though statements by the board and Steinhafel indicated they had reached a mutual agreement. In a proxy Target filed with the

US Securities and Exchange Commission, Steinhafel's exit was called "an involuntary termination for reasons other than for cause." Target did not further elaborate on the explanation when asked by media members.[18]

" However, Target had also grown somewhat stale on Steinhafel's watch. Stores had expanded their food offerings, ostensibly to attract more shoppers, who would arrive to pick up a dozen eggs and then venture into the other parts of the store to make a higher-priced purchase, like a pair of designer jeans. But that strategy wasn't working.

Steinhafel's biggest sin had been being the guy in charge during a pair of crisis situations. Quicker action on his part following the data breach would have improved his chances of surviving. On the other hand, Target's struggles in Canada had left a large stain on his tenure.

Steinhafel had been the face of Target, so his departure helped sell Target customers on the idea that the company was doing everything possible to fix its problems.

"It became very apparent internally that we had to do something different if we wanted to succeed in the next ten years."

—MELISSA KREMER,
Target Executive Vice President

CHAPTER TWELVE

NEW LEADERSHIP

In the aftermath of Gregg Steinhafel's departure, Target continued to flounder in Canada while nursing the black eye incurred from its security breach. Melissa Kremer, executive vice president and chief human resources officer for Target, joined the company in 2004 as a recruiter. Today, she leads all aspects of human resources for Target's global team of 350,000 team members, from recruitment, development, and diversity and inclusion to engagement and total rewards. She recalled Target's climate post Steinhafel, noting, "It became very apparent internally that we had to do something different if we wanted to succeed in the next ten years."

"And so, you had an organization, quite frankly, that was ready for change," Kremer said.[1]

Help from the Outside

Target's board hired the search firm of Korn Ferry to find Steinhafel's successor. That decision loomed as one of the more important decisions in the company's history. Given its weight, speculation arose that Target might even try to bring back Robert Ulrich, who, at seventy, had not led the company since retiring at Target's mandated retirement age of sixty-five.

Credit the board for recognizing that the company needed a jolt, somebody who would not have skewed judgment influenced by years of seeing only good in the Bullseye. On July 31, 2014, Target announced that they had hired Brian Cornell to become chairman of the board and CEO.

Roxanne S. Austin, interim non-executive chair of Target's board, addressed Cornell's hiring in a company release: "As we seek to aggressively move Target forward and establish the company as a top omnichannel retailer, we focused on identifying an extraordinary leader who could bring vision, focus and a wealth of experience to Target's transformation. The Board is confident that Brian's diverse and broad experience in retail and consumer products as well as his passion for leading high performing teams will propel Target forward."[2]

In the same release, Cornell said: "I am honored and humbled to join Target as the first CEO hired from outside the company. I am committed to empowering this talented team to realize its full potential, lead change and strengthen the love guests have for this brand. As we create the Target of tomorrow, I will focus on our current business performance in both the US and Canada and on how we accelerate our omnichannel transformation."

Cornell left his position as CEO of PepsiCo Americas Foods to join Target. He had also served as president and CEO of

Walmart's Sam's Club division and he'd served as CEO of Michaels Stores, and chief marketing officer at Safeway. Specifically, Cornell had demonstrated skills for improving sales in the food and consumer basics categories.[3]

Cornell's hiring bucked tradition. The company's leadership had always been groomed from within and those leaders had always managed to successfully move the company forward. Target's management and excellence were synonymous. The company had long embraced the concept of "organizational surplus." Executives were expected to train their successors so there would be a seamless transition if the executive got promoted or retired. The process bred loyalty and stability within the ranks, building a team of executives well versed in the "Target Way." Never before had Target reached outside the Target family for a leader to run the show. Hiring an outsider represented a radical change that became necessary when the company boat began to sink, leaving Target in the precarious position of trying to stay afloat amid trying circumstances.

> " Hiring an outsider represented a radical change that became necessary when the company boat began to sink, leaving Target in the precarious position of trying to stay afloat amid trying circumstances.

Mulligan wasn't surprised at the board's decision. "The fact that I was the interim CEO, after being the CFO for maybe a year and a half, meant there probably wasn't anybody internally [to fill the post]. Didn't mean there wasn't any talent. Because dating all the way back to when I got here, the thing that has remained the same, we are fortunate we have great talent. So there was great talent, but nobody was ready for that job."[4]

Just a Boy Growing Up in Queens

Cornell experienced a tough childhood growing up in Queens, New York. His parents split when he was young, leaving his mother and maternal grandparents to raise him. His mother had "major health issues" according to Cornell, who elaborated by saying that she had "major heart surgery [at a time] when that didn't happen very often"—a condition that restricted her ability to work and left the family to get by on her disability checks, circumstances that directed Cornell to develop a solid work ethic. From an early age, he sought work, performing any number of jobs to earn money.

Doctors told Cornell's mother that her chances of living a longer life would be enhanced by living in a moderate climate. That prompted a move from New York to Los Angeles.

Sports had been an indulgence of Cornell's youth, and he'd become a UCLA fan, even though he'd grown up in Queens. "I was, literally, always a UCLA fan," Cornell remembered. "I grew up when there was one game of the week—it was a CBS game with Dick Enberg. And, most Saturdays, it was UCLA playing [basketball], because it was the heyday of John Wooden. I grew up as a UCLA fan, back in those days in Queens. And it was kind of a dream to go to UCLA."[5] Cornell idolized Wooden, the famed UCLA basketball coach, particularly because of his penchant for paying attention to even the smallest of details.

Cornell continued to work odd jobs while pursuing a bachelor's degree at UCLA that he earned in 1981. Ten years later, he continued his education by enrolling in UCLA's Anderson School of Management.

While CEO of Sam's Club from 2009 to 2012, Cornell oversaw initiatives and changes that brought improved outcomes to Walmart's membership warehouse club division. Just prior to joining Target, he served as the chief executive of PepsiCo Americas Foods (a division that includes Frito-Lay North America, Quaker Foods, and PepsiCo's Latin American food and snack businesses)—the year after he joined, PepsiCo enjoyed $25 billion in sales.[6] That same year, the unit's sales improved by 5 percent after increasing by 4 percent in 2012, Cornell's first year at PepsiCo.[7]

Cornell valued analytics, an appreciation gained during his days at Safeway when he used data from an upgraded analytics department to improve its Lifestyle stores. Analytics had also benefited him at Sam's Club, where he used them to help improve its customer-insights system.[8] Cornell's appreciation for analytics appealed to Target's board, as did his reputation as a leader and his proven ability to build private-label brands. He understood the worth of having the right culture, and had a history of successfully creating it.

> Cornell's appreciation for analytics appealed to Target's board, as did his reputation as a leader and his proven ability to build private-label brands. He understood the worth of having the right culture, and had a history of successfully creating it.

Cornell had served on the board at Polaris since 2012. Polaris CEO Scott Wine said of Cornell in a *Star Tribune* article: "He doesn't need to be the loudest one in the room, but he often has the most important thing to say."[9]

Not everybody agreed that Cornell was the correct choice. *Forbes* ran a story titled, "Target's New CEO Brian Cornell Lacks Innovative Pizzazz." In the story, Walter Loeb wrote, "Target's transformation will take some time. None of [Cornell's] background at other companies assures us that he has the mettle to innovate."[10]

Rick Gomez is executive vice president, chief marketing and digital officer for Target, and a member of its executive leadership team. He acknowledged that when a new leader comes aboard, there is always "a little bit of ambiguity, people are asking questions, and there's change, [but] I think the overall sense was we were excited to have someone of Brian's caliber coming into the CEO role," Gomez said. "The business wasn't performing well. We knew we needed to drive change. I think there was a real openness to him. When you look at his background, coming from retail, coming from real iconic brands. I knew he had worked in marketing. He had an appreciation for the role that marketing plays. The importance of building loyalty. Of building brand love. Those were all good things. I think there was a little bit of, 'What does this mean for me?' And, 'What kind of change is going to come?' But I think, in general, we knew we needed to change."[11]

Still, Cornell arrived at Target "recognizing that there would be a lot of questions."

"People were questioning why we went to the outside," Cornell said. "Who is Brian Cornell? What am I going to bring to the business?"

Cornell conceded that his acceptance probably had been accelerated by his arrival during "a challenging time for the company." "We were still recovering from the data breach," Cornell said. "We had a business in Canada that was failing. Our core US performance had been lagging for a few years. So timing was actually my friend, because the company was willing to step back and say, 'Okay, we've got to make changes. Because what we're doing right now is not producing the results we were looking for.'"[12]

Target's board felt a change of culture was needed to improve results going forward. The following areas most needed to be addressed at the time:

- US sales: Same-store sales is a financial metric used by retailers for evaluating the total dollar amount of sales in the company's stores that have been operating for a year or more. Target had experienced dips in same-store sales in the United States in three of the previous five quarters.
- Digital: Target had not kept pace in the digital world, so ramping up in that arena needed to be a priority. Along those same lines, the chain needed to become an "omnichannel" retailer by giving customers choices for shopping in addition to traditional brick-and-mortar stores, including shopping through smartphone apps and internet browsers. Target had outsourced its online sales platform to Amazon prior to launching a website and taking control of its online sales. Though Target.com had been well intended, they still lagged behind where e-commerce was concerned. Target had found some success,

however, with its "Cartwheel" mobile app, which
enabled customers to find deals that could be applied
at checkout.

▪ Merchandising: Target's merchandising needed a
boost. New items had dropped from 56 percent of
Target's total assortment in 2006 to 34 percent in
2013.[13]

▪ Canada: Should the corporation continue in Canada
or would it be best to shut down the operation to
avoid further losses?

▪ Smaller stores: At that point, just 12 percent of
Target's stores were in urban areas, putting them far
behind Walmart in that category.

▪ The data breach: Earning back the trust of Target
customers after the ordeal remained a priority.

Cornell cited the data breach and the struggles in Canada as
being a "part of why we're here. It allowed us to step back and
say, 'We've got to think differently. We need to understand
where we are, from a capability standpoint, from a strategy
standpoint.' And it allowed our leadership team and the board
to step back and say, 'We've got to reassess the business.'"[14]

"The competition was moving past us. The consumer had changed. And we were still admiring the things that we did for so long so well."

—**BRIAN CORNELL,** Target CEO

CHAPTER THIRTEEN

THE CLEANUP BEGINS

During Brian Cornell's first days on the job, he addressed employees in a town hall–style meeting, talked to company suppliers, and flew to Canada to get a firsthand look at Target's ongoing disaster. Ever the optimist, Cornell told the *Star Tribune*, "I'm absolutely convinced that the best for Target is yet to come."[1]

Cornell carried a much more visible public persona than his closely guarded predecessors—Bob Ulrich he was not. From the get-go, he established a calmer climate in the corporate office, one less about having an unapproachable autocrat in an ivory tower than a head man who embraced ideas and communication. To that end, he relaxed the dress code and he often ate in the company cafeteria, talking to employees like a regular Joe. He preferred to be transparent about his intentions, like the ones he shared on September 10, 2014, during the annual company gathering of 14,000 employees held at the Target Center. Managers from 1,800 stores are flown into

Minneapolis for the annual meeting. They learn about new strategies, merchandise, and advertising. That year, Taylor Swift and Jamie Foxx performed, as did the British group Coldplay. And Cornell spoke, telling his audience that Target needed "to be cool again," stressing that one of his initial priorities was to reestablish Target's reputation for style by focusing on home, apparel, baby, and beauty products.[2]

Cornell knew all about Target and its history, and had "tremendous respect for the brand and the relationship the brand had with the guests that we served." "But I quickly recognized that we had become a bit insular in our focus," Cornell said. "[That we had] not spent enough time thinking about the changes in the external environment. How the consumer was changing. How the guest was changing. How the competition had evolved. And I think we spent a lot more time saying, 'All right, we've got to be thinking about the external environment and really assessing how the consumer, the competition, our own guest was changing. And, how do we adapt to this new model?'"[3]

Cornell believed past success worked against Target to a certain extent. "We had been, as a company, so successful for so long. And, I've used this analogy a couple of times, but we had a lot of trophies in the cabinets."

Dusting Off the Trophies

Target had been recognized for being the best in merchandising, retail, marketing, in-store experience, and supply chain. "And, we had all those trophies stacked up year after year, and all of a sudden, they got a little tarnished, because we were celebrating the wins of the past," Cornell said. "But the competition was moving past us. The consumer had changed. And we were still admiring the things that we did for so long so well."[4]

> And, we had all those trophies stacked up year after year, and all of a sudden, they got a little tarnished, because we were celebrating the wins of the past," Cornell said. "But the competition was moving past us. The consumer had changed. And we were still admiring the things that we did for so long so well."

Target stopped getting trophies, forcing them to step back and take an inventory of where they were in relation to the consumer and the competition, and to assess where changes were needed.

John Mulligan, who became COO, complimented Cornell for the way he went about his business, being "respectful of Target's culture and where it came from. But also saying, 'Hey, there's some stuff we're going to have to change,'" Mulligan said. "'Not only about the way we operate the business, but about the culture. There are some things we're going to have to tweak.' And I think he just did that really masterfully."[5]

Cornell had to select his management team, being sensitive to the possibility of creating animosity by hiring from outside the Target family. Conversely, selecting too many candidates from within the Target family could have perpetuated the existing climate. Cornell opted to make selections from both the outside and the inside.

"I knew that there was going to be great talent in the organization," Cornell said. "It was finding the right mix of people who had great institutional knowledge, and where we needed to go to the outside.

"We needed to enhance our technology skills. We needed to embrace the digital environment. So we brought some new people in. But if you look at my leadership team today, there's a really interesting blend of people who have been here for years and years. Great institutional knowledge. And others that we brought on board to help us redefine the direction of the company."[6]

Rick Gomez, who is now Target's chief marketing officer, called Cornell "the best kind of boss" because he "is a predictable boss. He's consistent. You know what's important to him, and he's consistent on that. There are no surprises," Gomez said. "That hasn't been challenging. It's easy to read him, and you know what he's looking for."[7]

Gomez appreciated how Cornell let people do their jobs without micromanaging. "The fact that he was a CMO at one point in his career could be a good thing, right? He understands the value of marketing. It could also be a bad thing, because he's done the role and likes marketing. But he does not get involved in the day to day on the marketing stuff at all. He has a high level of trust. And I think if he feels like the work is good, and is delivering what the objectives are, and it's driving the business, that's not what he's going to focus on."

Cornell recognized the importance of Target's social command center, which monitored live feeds from social media channels and used software to bring critical data to light. He ramped up this department, and looked for additional ways to use data to better Target.[8]

Getting Out of Canada

Unannounced store visits became a part of Cornell's hands-on approach—he'd ask customers questions and observe how everything operated. The visits he paid to several Montreal stores the Saturday before Christmas were eye-opening. Normally, a shoehorn would have been needed to fit shoppers inside—it's one of the busiest retail days of the year. But Cornell found just the opposite, and it proved to be the tipping point for making a critical decision.[9] Three weeks after those visits, Cornell decided Target needed to get out of Canada.

On January 15, 2015, Target announced that it had begun orchestrating its exodus. Cornell answered questions about the move in the company blog, where he said: "The losses were just too great. Given that the holiday season is our busiest time of the year, we evaluated our fourth quarter performance carefully and unfortunately didn't see the step change in our performance we needed to see. I know that the Canadian team worked as hard as any team possibly could have to turn things around. I have witnessed first-hand their tireless work and determination to improve Target Canada's performance, and our decision in no way diminishes their tremendous efforts."[10]

Results and projections backed the decision. Target had lost almost $1 billion in its first year in Canada and had spent approximately $7 billion on the Canada operation. Though the losses were no longer coming at the same rate that Target had initially experienced, they were still losing money daily. Cornell rationalized that Target had ventured into a "very" competitive market and "hadn't spent enough time understanding the needs of that Canadian consumer." For example, the requirements for success in Quebec were different than they were in Vancouver.

"And ultimately, we disappointed that Canadian consumer," Cornell said. "They had very high expectations for the brand. Many of them had shopped Target when they were in the US. And actually, the net promoter scores were off the charts. And their expectations were really high. And we disappointed."

Projections told Cornell that the Canadian operation would not get to a point of breaking even until 2021 or 2022. "Which means we were going to distract our organization for years," Cornell said. "It was going to require a lot more capital. And I looked at where we were at that point, and I said we're going to double down on the US. Make sure we're not distracted by a challenged Canadian business."[11]

Target shut down 133 Canadian stores with 17,600 employees. Cornell called the move the "most difficult personal, and business, decision I ever had to make."

 Target shut down 133 Canadian stores with 17,600 employees. Cornell called the move the "most difficult personal, and business, decision I ever had to make."

Cornell believed Target had dropped the ball by biting off too much initially. He recognized the operational challenges. "Our stores struggled with inventory issues and we were not as sharp on pricing as we should have been, which led to pricing perception issues. As a result, we delivered an experience that didn't meet our guests' expectations, or our own. Unfortunately, the negative guest sentiment became too much to overcome."[12]

Exiting Canada was a dire move that affected many. But gloom and doom about Target's future didn't follow. Many in the financial industry saluted the decision to cut loose an albatross. Mark Miller, an analyst at the Chicago-based investment bank William Blair & Co., wrote in a note to clients shared in *Chain Drug Review*: "The good news is that Target will stop throwing good money after bad. The bad news is that Target's long-term growth opportunity is now effectively limited to the United States."[13]

Target created a $70-million trust to help employees affected by the shutdown while they looked for other opportunities. It allowed Canadian employees to receive a minimum of sixteen weeks of compensation, including wages and benefits.

Cornell remained optimistic about Target's future. "We are encouraged by the early momentum we see in our US business but we know the retail landscape is constantly evolving. At Target, this means we have to thoughtfully focus and prioritize the guest like never before. We need to work in new ways, we need to further invest in our top priorities and make strategic decisions related to expense. In other words, we have to transform our business for long-term growth. And there is no question, we will."[14]

"There's a lot of work that goes into making sure [the stores] feel navigable and clean and bright."

—JOHN MULLIGAN, Target COO

CHAPTER FOURTEEN

ADDING DIRECTION

Brian Cornell revealed his vision about Target's direction during its investor conference on March 3, 2015. He outlined a strategy that would emphasize the following going forward:

- Embracing omnichannel retailing.
- Concentrating on the signature categories.
- Tailoring assortments to local needs and tastes and personalizing the only shopping experience for Target guests.
- Focusing on urban store formats.
- Cutting costs.[1]

Cornell offered an explanation for his priorities in an article that appeared in *MMR* (*Mass Market Retailers*). "As we focus our resources on making progress in these key priorities, we expect to accelerate top-line growth by driving traffic to our existing stores by elevating signature categories, enhancing our guests' digital engagement with Target, becoming more localized and personalized, and ensuring we provide a great in-store experience. We want to ensure our guests can shop on demand by enhancing our mobile and supply chain capabilities, leading to growth in our digital sales, and by thoughtfully growing our store base, particularly these urban formats, like CityTarget and TargetExpress, to further elevate the overall Target brand."[2]

Defining the Target Customer

Target sprang into action. Defining the Target customer became a priority. Rick Gomez was responsible for leading marketing efforts across all merchandise categories. Recalling the Target climate when he came aboard, Gomez observed, "I think we lost sight of who we were and who we are as a brand. We had lost sight of who our guest was and how our guest had changed."[3]

Target's perceived composite customer had always been a white suburban mom, who had two kids and drove a minivan. "And that is a big part of who our guests are, but the reality is, our guest has increasingly become more millennial, Gen Z," Gomez said. "And has become more multicultural. Urban. So, we have a much broader definition, or perspective, of who our guest is than I think we had five or six years ago."[4]

Target set a goal to become more "guest-centric," or to put the store's guests first. The marketing department used quantitative studies, focus groups, and home visits to gain insights about consumers. Deep immersions would see Target executives spend significant amounts of time visiting consumers' homes.[5] Gomez was one of them. "We asked [consumers] about their brands and where they shopped. I've sat through conversations going through a makeup bag for four hours, talking about makeup and beauty. And [with women] I've gone through their closet, [discovered] what she thinks about her outfits and her shopping. Pantries, medicine cabinets."[6]

> **Deep immersions would see Target executives spend significant amounts of time visiting consumers' homes. Gomez was one of them. "We asked [consumers] about their brands and where they shopped. I've sat through conversations going through a makeup bag for four hours, talking about makeup and beauty."**

Most of the C-suite invested time in these visits, a fact Gomez called "critical" to the exercise. "And you get a whole new perspective, and you start to build empathy [for the customer]," Gomez said.[7]

Cornell strongly believed that defining the Target customer would go a long way toward understanding the path Target needed to travel to find future success. Cornell made his share of home visits and observed that he learned a lot about Target's customers in terms of what they liked and disliked, and how they lived.

"Here's the way retail fits into their lives," Cornell said. "What they're looking for today, and what we can make sure we're including in our offering to capture more of their footsteps, or more clicks, depending on how they're shopping."[8]

For example, Target gained a keener understanding about how young mothers shopped for baby products and how important trust and brands were to them and what they were looking for. That "allowed us to alter some of our assortment," Cornell said. "Think about how we merchandise differently. But it really forced us to double down on the importance of moms to our brands. And if you think about the hundreds and hundreds of Target stories that are out there, so many of them are tied to young moms. Talking about the fact they bought their first car seat at Target and their first diapers and children's clothing. And that evolved into shopping for toys. And while they were there, they discovered other household essentials and things that they liked in our assortment for their homes. And they started shopping for themselves. But our brand has been connected to moms and families for years."[9]

Cornell credited the home visits for reminding everyone that Target served real families and real people.[10]

A Little Less Insulation

Target embarked on a major restructuring. By the end of 2015, Target and CVS Health completed a deal for Target to sell its pharmacy and clinical businesses to CVS for approximately $1.9 billion. All told, that equated to 1,672 pharmacies in forty-seven states that would begin to operate as a store-within-a-store format.

Target's ensuing partnership with CVS Health allowed Target to maintain its focus by concentrating on its core business while also affording customers a convenient, and legitimate, place to take care of their health-care and pharmacy needs. In addition, the sale generated cash and allowed the company to leave the drugstore business, a field that required escalating resources to remain competitive.

In early March of 2015, 1,700 employees were informed that their jobs were being eliminated, a move that would allow the company to save $2 billion in costs over a two-year period. The downsizing also aimed to create a leaner, more efficient management team.[11]

> In early March of 2015, 1,700 employees were informed that their jobs were being eliminated, a move that would allow the company to save $2 billion in costs over a two-year period. The downsizing also aimed to create a leaner, more efficient management team.

Creating a system where managers could work cross functionally became a part of Cornell's plan. Teams had long been isolated, working within their separate silos.

"In the past you could easily make decisions within your function. Today, because the guest experience is so multidimensional, those decisions have to happen across functions," Kremer said.

"Think about the assortment that we should sell on Target. com. That has to be a decision that merchandising and the digital folks are making. How we get that product to the guest has to not only be a decision that digital is making, but supply chain and stores have to make that decision too. So, it's such a multidimensional guest journey different than five or six years ago."[12]

The Importance of Supply Chain

John Mulligan's move from interim CEO to COO put supply chain under his command. It is the backbone of any good retailer. According to the Council of Supply Chain Management Professionals, the supply chain refers to the resources needed to deliver goods and services to a consumer. Not surprisingly, supply chain management is an integral part of most businesses and is essential to company success and customer satisfaction.

Myriad problems might result from having a flawed supply chain, like the empty shelves Target experienced in Canada. Target's supply chain had grown old, and it was showing cracks from aging. "We grew up from a department store; I think we looked at the supply chain like department stores," Mulligan said.[13]

Target had done a "great job ensuring we always had capacity" according to Mulligan. However, Target's supply chain was complex, due primarily to the variety of products served.

"We run five businesses, and they're all about even [in importance]," said Mulligan, rattling off the five to include food and beverage; essentials and beauty; hardlines; apparel; and home. "All of those are very different."

And Target did not lead with one category like most retailers. Even Walmart—which had a diverse portfolio like Target—

was led by food. "Sixty percent of their business is food, so you can build a supply chain around food, and kind of everything else will come along for the ride," Mulligan said. "The needs for apparel are very different than fresh food. And toys is very different, because 70 percent of your sales come in Q4. That requires a different supply chain."

Target had done well in building a supply chain that could adapt to handling the variety. However, Mulligan added: "We just kind of stopped innovating around it, and building the next new thing and learning."[14] Mulligan said Target had gotten "to a place where we were copying, copying, and copying."

"That's what we did year after year," Mulligan said. "And then we got to a place a decade, a decade and a half later, and we were like, 'Uh, the world's moved a little bit on us. And so, we need to iterate and update what we're doing.'"[15]

The supply chain management team that Target had in place lacked expertise in "a few areas of supply chain" according to Mulligan. "We needed to bring in some people. We wanted to build a high-performing team. We set out to do that, and that took some time."[16] Target measured the performance metrics for its supply chain against the best in its class. "Cycle time, speed of delivery, accuracy, inventory positioning," Mulligan said. "We had gaps across all of that."[17]

Direct-to-guest fulfillment and replenishment became priorities. Mulligan said there are three key elements for replenishment: "Reduce out of stocks. Improve the total labor—that means take labor hours out of back of the store so they can focus on spending time with the guests. . . . Third, free up space in the back room. And the back room was all about direct-to-guest fulfillment."[18]

The ideal of facilitating continued improvement guided the decision making. "The team has worked hard on technology,"

Mulligan said. "We've worked hard on our transportation. We've worked hard on our cycle times. There's some automation we're using. I think the team has made great progress working on all of those, but I think it all started with getting the right team and bringing in some expertise that we didn't have when we started."[19]

Cleanup in Aisle 6

Making sure the inventory didn't clutter the stores with messy aisles or unpackaged product remained a priority. "Make sure the store looks great," Mulligan said. "Make sure it's guest ready. Make sure guests feel welcome when they're in there. . . . There's a lot of work that goes into making sure [the stores] feel navigable and clean and bright."[20]

Target took measures to improve its performance in the digital arena, such as using digital technology to enhance the customer's in-store experience, experimenting with methods to speed up shipping on digital orders, and improving its mobile experience—simplifying in-store navigation.

Because ramping up its digital business and improving its supply chain required expertise, Target turned its hiring focus toward tech operations and bringing aboard analytics specialists and engineers. Kremer led the HR strategy for Target's omnichannel initiative with the awareness that the future of retail was about brick-and-mortar shopping as well as the digital experience online.

"We knew at that point we fundamentally did not have the right talent, the right capabilities, or the right structure for the organization," said Kremer, noting that she began working on a human capital strategy that would equip Target with the right culture, the right talent, and the right capabilities needed to deliver on an omnichannel experience.

"At that point we realized to deliver on an omnichannel journey, we needed to invest in supply chain," Kremer said. "We needed to invest in data and analytics. And we needed to invest in technology and engineering. And we didn't have all that talent in house. So we went to the market to find some world-class leaders in those spaces that brought the expertise and they brought the network. And that helped us start to unlock access to other talent pools that then helped us accelerate the build-out of those capabilities that were really central to our strategy to delivering for the guests."[21]

Accordingly, Target ramped up operations in Bangalore, India, locale of "Target in India," where every business area at Target had representatives.[22]

Set up in 2005, Target in India would grow to more than three thousand employees engaged in work that supported Target across business areas such as technology, marketing, human resources, finance, merchandising, supply chain, property development, analytics, and reporting.[23]

Brian Cornell, the outsider, had delivered the goods, bringing clarity on strategy, a focus on Target's purpose as an organization, and he'd begun to galvanize the organization around strategy, priorities, and purpose. But Cornell's auspicious beginning could never have prepared anyone for what would follow.

"They want newness.
They want great style
and value. And they want
customer service."

—**BRIAN CORNELL,** Target CEO

BRICK-AND-MORTAR RETAIL NOT DEAD

Brick-and-mortar retail appeared to be dead. Amazon and e-commerce had won the war. Perception said traditional retail shopping outlets, where customers walked aisles and perused merchandise, had gone the way of newspapers and pay phones.

Target's stores had once been places of joy, where customers were constantly surprised by the offerings and reasonable prices. By 2017, most of those stores were now outdated and had devolved into functional retailers that lacked luster. Target found itself at a crossroads. Its stores obviously needed to be renovated, but why invest money in renovations when brick-and-mortar retail was dead?

"The only person who wasn't asked [whether brick-and-mortar retail was dead] was the actual core consumer, who still likes to shop physical retail," Cornell said.[1]

The Wharton School of the University of Pennsylvania and the NPD Group Inc., a global information firm, performed a study in which NPD Group's Checkout Tracking system tracked receipts from the online and brick-and-mortar retail purchases of fifty thousand consumers from January 2015 to June 2015.

> **Target found itself at a crossroads. Its stores obviously needed to be renovated, but why invest money in renovations when brick-and-mortar retail was dead?**

Unsurprisingly, the survey showed that millennials made more purchases through e-commerce, backing the idea that brick-and-mortar was really being disrupted. However, that same study indicated that mass merchants, including Target and Walmart, were popular with the young shoppers. Target's focus on online and mobile channels had been a factor in that popularity.[2]

Breathing New Life into Brick-and-Mortar

Addressing the state of Target's brick-and-mortar inventory, Brian Cornell announced a radical plan on February 28, 2017. Target would spend $2 billion in 2017, and a total of more than $7 billion over the course of three years. The plan included price reductions, launching more private label brands, opening more smaller-format stores, and remodeling stores.[3]

Approximately 100 stores were to be remodeled in 2017, followed by another 250 in 2018, with a goal of having 600 of

Target's 1,800 stores "reimagined" by 2019 and 1,000 by the end of 2020. Each remodel would come at an approximate cost of $3–$5 million with an estimated return of a 2–4 percent increase in sales in those stores.

> Approximately 100 stores were to be remodeled in 2017, followed by another 250 in 2018, with a goal of having 600 of Target's 1,800 stores "reimagined" by 2019 and 1,000 by the end of 2020. Each remodel would come at an approximate cost of $3–$5 million with an estimated return of a 2–4 percent increase in sales in those stores.

Target also planned to increase its inventory of smaller-format stores in densely populated urban areas. The goal was to have more than one hundred of these stores by 2019. Cornell firmly believed the consumer liked to do his or her shopping in a physical store. "But they expect a great in-store experience," Cornell said. "They want newness. They want great style and value. And they want customer service. And that's what we identified when we laid out our strategy."[4]

Remodeling stores?! The decision to invest in the chain's physical stores when brick-and-mortar had purportedly died was the most curious piece of Target's new plan. Had Cornell flipped his lid? Going all in with brick-and-mortar sounded like going back to the telegraph. The previous twelve months had already seen Target's stock drop 29 percent.[5]

"I'm in New York, and we push the button with our press release," Cornell recalled. "And I'm in my hotel room watching CNBC. After we pushed the button, Becky Quick was reading, and she says, 'Target's going to invest $7 billion of capital. A billion dollars of operating income in their stores and in their team.' She said, 'There must be a typo. Nobody would be investing these kinds of numbers. There must be a mistake. We'll get back to them.'

"I'm watching our stock price in the pre-market in a steep decline. A couple of hours later, I had to get onstage in front of hundreds of investors and the steps looked about this big."[6] Cornell used his hand to illustrate a step that would have been four feet above the floor, then smiled. "But we had confidence that we were doing the right things for the long term. We knew it was going to be a tough day. I didn't know it was going to be that tough. I ended my day by doing a live CNBC interview, which ended effectively with: 'Brian, how long do you think you have in this job?'"[7]

Cornell addressed Target investors and employees that week, facing "a lot of team members" who wondered why Target had gone off the tracks in a direction that Wall Street questioned, and one that had the media shaking their heads.

"We had to make sure we brought our entire team along and change the culture, to say, 'Here's how we're going to operate differently, here's why we're going to do this, here's why long term this is going to pay off,'" Cornell said. "But when we announced it, there were a lot of headlines saying Target is taking a very different approach than everyone else. And questioned why.

"Why would we be investing in stores when everyone is writing about stores going away? Why would we invest in our team when people are trying to cut costs and just get from quarter to quarter? There were a lot of people who thought we had kind of lost our way."

Though the market did not react well—and Cornell heard from plenty of skeptics across the board that fateful day—he received some positive feedback too. "I actually had several investors come up to me and say, 'Brian, if I was in your job, I'd do the exact same thing. I'd be investing for the long term. I'd be building those new capabilities. I'd be investing in your stores, and in fulfillment, and digital capabilities, and your team. So you're doing the right thing. You just have to make sure you bring the investment community along. You [need to] put proof points on the board every quarter.'"[8]

Cornell's strategy had not been a knee-jerk reaction to dwindling profits. Target had dipped its toe in the water long before jumping in. Target's earlier exercise of making in-home visits had paid dividends, and Cornell noted that much of the plan had been "driven by my internal team." By getting to know their customer, Target had learned that their customers still wanted the brick-and-mortar experience. "We did a lot of work going inside of homes," Cornell said. "In-store discussions. We spent a lot of time talking to consumers."[9]

Even though Target had done a lot of testing before moving to action at scale, Cornell conceded, "We laid out a very ambitious plan. There were a lot of people shaking their heads saying, 'Now wait a minute, they're going to put billions of dollars into physical stores? Stores are dying. They're actually going to build new small stores. Well, people aren't shopping in those stores. They're going to use their stores as distribution hubs when others are building DCs upstream, and you're going to pay your team higher wages? What are you thinking of?'"[10]

A Bold, New Direction: LA25

Target traveled a different path than its competition, but it was a path paved with consumer research. "It was called a bold, new direction. But we had taken the consumer as a partner along the way and felt confident that we were doing the right thing for the brand, not just for the long term, but to make sure this brand is still a prominent player in retail thirty years from now."[11]

Unlike Canada, where Target went big all at once—and failed big—Target had been experimenting with remodeling concepts beginning in 2016, using the Los Angeles market as a proving ground. They instituted a pilot program called "LA25." Twenty-five stores were equipped with thirty-five store enhancements that had been tested across the country. Among the enhancements were a better-lit fresh produce section, dedicated service stations where customers could quickly pick up online orders, and sleeker apparel fixtures. The pilots also employed service advisers who could help customers navigate Target's website and its mobile app, Cartwheel.

The Los Angeles area was chosen because it housed a variety of Target stores, including several of the smaller-market format.[12] "We iterated from there," Cornell said.[13]

Research had told Target that consumers were moving from the suburbs back to city centers. These small-format stores were developed on or near college campuses, in large cities, and, generally, at any locale lacking the space for a regular-sized Target. In addition to offering products that fit the local population at affordable prices, the small-format stores delivered a place for

Target.com orders to be picked up. "We had to learn how to operate a smaller store, because we were used to a hundred-plus thousand feet," Cornell said. "Now we're operating in twenty, thirty, or forty thousand square feet. We started with a handful of those and started to learn how to sort differently, how to replenish those stores, how to operate in these new urban environments, or on college campuses. We went from ten stores to now we have a hundred, but we had a test along the way."

Replenishing the small stores brought challenges. Target addressed those challenges and what they learned helped bring solutions to the larger stores, too, helping them become more efficient. For example, dramatically shrinking the store's back rooms to create more floor space for sales. They also focused on improving their assortment so that they had capacity on the floor for items with high-volume sales.[14]

John Mulligan cited Tide as an example of a high-volume item. "If you're going to sell a lot of Tide, make sure you have a capacity of Tide. We had to change how often we replenish in those stores. Some [of the small stores] get five deliveries a day. Some actually get seven a day. Changes had to be made since we'd never delivered that often."[15]

Also, as part of Cornell's February 28, 2017, announcement, Target revealed plans to roll out more than twelve new brands—primarily in home and apparel. The Cat & Jack and the Pillowfort brands had launched in 2016 and found great success.

"We knew our brand portfolio had gotten a little tired," Cornell said. "And we started with [Cat & Jack], which was our first reinvention, that is now a multibillion-dollar brand, and we've followed that path in style and essential categories with a number of new brands. And those have connected with the consumer and our guests, but a lot of things we had to test and learn along the way."[16]

A Merchandising Makeover

Target had already begun a merchandising makeover at the time of Cornell's announcement. Target sought to solve the merchandising puzzle of how they could move customers from one product to another. For example, if a customer came into the store to buy groceries, how could they entice them to also visit apparel or home? What were the trigger points?

> " Target sought to solve the merchandising puzzle of how they could move customers from one product to another. For example, if a customer came into the store to buy groceries, how could they entice them to also visit apparel or home?

Target's longtime guests knew how to shop there. But how should Target teach new customers to expect a little bit more out of Target when they came inside? Hired experts helped educate store managers and employees about visual merchandising. Target repurposed space next to the Minneapolis corporate office and used it to simulate a store. Seasoned Target personnel needed to learn how to think differently and embrace new ideas.

Target attacked product areas across the board: for example, "Project Lace" brought a strategic approach to intimate apparel, aimed at establishing a new environment for the Target brands Auden, Stars Above, and Colsie. At that time, Target's market share in the bra category sat at No. 5. Target thought improvements in this area were attainable—they saw it like picking low-hanging fruit—and so they set the goal of reaching the No. 3 spot.[17]

Target performed a makeover on the entire department, which began with simulations at the mock store in Minneapolis. That resulted in bringing an atmosphere to the intimates department that helped promote a more inspiring and easy-to-shop experience. Target realized that female shoppers did not want to feel exposed while shopping for bras, which prompted them to relocate bras away from the aisles. They also identified that frame and function ranked first in importance, followed by style, then size, and then having an easier shopping experience—which inspired Target to create an area that allowed the shopper to move about the entire perimeter of the bra section without having to bend down. Underwear and panties were mixed throughout, making it easier to match them with bras. Everything was integrated for simpler shopping online as well.

A visual merchandising team set up training and guidelines establishing the way Target should and should not present products, while staying true to their brand principles. Implementing the use of mannequins became a huge deal that required store associates and managers to learn how to use them to create eye-catching displays. Target wanted to ensure that handling the mannequins didn't become counterproductive. Mannequins weren't to be changed daily—after all, Target wasn't Bergdorf's or Barney's—so they weren't rotated until at least four weeks after being changed.

Target's home and seasonal side of the business worked ahead a year out, planning their presentations in the mock store.

Apparel relied more on virtual simulations, like computer-aided drawings where display environments were sketched in 3D.

Display designs in the mock store would be evaluated, revealing almost immediately whether or not a display would work through indicators that included the time required for a store team to set up the display, if employees could keep the display consistent, or if the display was simply too arduous to maintain. Every model that graduated from the mock store had been properly vetted. Iterations of displays were made based on how guests shopped it. Did they purchase? Did the store team have any observations on how the guests shopped it? Was it easy for them to get to a purchase? And, for the store teams, could they set up the display and maintain it?[18]

"Gondolas"—the normal aisles that run through Target stores in a linear fashion—were still a feature of the reimagined stores. But many changes contributed to a new look that enhanced the shopping experience. Shelves were lowered to improve sight lines, allowing shoppers to see farther into the store. Fresh food was placed in grower bins, creating an organic farm feel. And the "360 shopping experience" came into being.

Disney and Target Together

The Disney collaboration served as an example of how a "360 shopping experience" worked. In October of 2019, the Disney experience was set up in twenty-five select stores, in the space adjacent to the toy department. Inside the 360 space were interactive areas for kids, apparel, books, and Disney franchise pieces as well, affording kids a place to be entertained while their parents shopped.

The Disney experience required many questions to be answered, like: Which Disney products and stories were the big commodities? What were the right stories to feature in the space? What lead story did they want to tell? For example, the Disney rollout inside Target went heavy on merchandise from *Frozen 2* and *Star Wars: The Rise of Skywalker*.

Target's partnering with Walt Disney to launch Disney stores within Target stores displayed an enlightened state of creativity. What better way for Target to leverage its brand than by having an association with Disney?

Building on its partnership with Disney, Target will open a new store near the Walt Disney World Resort in Orlando, Florida. Target also has planned additional Disney stores within a store in coming years. Target's website now features a Disney-Themed section. No doubt, Target will look to bring on board similarly strong partners in the future.

The Cornell Verdict

A little more than a year after Cornell introduced his bold improvement plan, Target had successfully lowered prices, redesigned stores, expanded its exclusive brands, enhanced its online business, and opened smaller stores near college campuses and in big cities. Target's stock responded with a 47 percent gain.[19] By August of 2019, Target had posted eight consecutive quarters of comparable sales increases.

Target's design team has continued to develop new brands—some of which have been huge successes. Collaborations with celebrities like Chip and Joanna Gaines from the reality TV show *Fixer Upper* have added to that success. Joanna has made visits to Target's home location in Minneapolis to work with the presentation team, the product design team, and the merchants.

Not only do in-house brands bring better profit margins, they bring into the store customers who are curious to discover Target's next surprise.

Target has realized another one of Cornell's initial goals by offering customers a legitimate omnichannel experience, which has in turn enhanced the customer's sales experience. Customers can now make purchases through a mobile app, a desktop application, or a brick-and-mortar store.

Competing with Amazon

In December of 2017, Target paid $550 million to buy Shipt, an online same-day delivery service. The acquisition has helped Target compete with Amazon by combining its network of stores with Shipt's technology platform and shopper community to offer customers a personalized same-day delivery option. By the end of 2019, Shipt had the capacity to deliver 65,000 Target items in as soon as an hour by shopping approximately 1,500 stores in forty-eight states.[20]

Other Target same-day fulfillment services include Drive-Up, where a Target employee will bring a customer's order to their car; and Order Pickup, where the customer can go inside the store to pick up their order.

Making Target a fun place to shop continues to be a huge part of the equation. The company has cultivated the idea that Target is a destination, successfully reigniting "Tar-zhay."

Throughout, Target has continued to think about the customer first. "We've spent several years now saying, 'When we make decisions, is it the right thing for the families we serve each and every day?'" Cornell said. "With 85 percent of America shopping Target during the year, we're a very inclusive brand. We're very family focused. If we're delighting the family and we're doing the right thing from an in-store standpoint, a digital standpoint, and we're bringing them the right brands, the right value, and the right customer service, if they feel good about it, ultimately, we thought, 'Shareholders will recognize that.' And we'll continue to see our performance improve."[21]

> " In December of 2017, Target paid $550 million to buy Shipt, an online same-day delivery service. The acquisition has helped Target compete with Amazon by combining its network of stores with Shipt's technology platform and shopper community to offer customers a personalized same-day delivery option. By the end of 2019, Shipt had the capacity to deliver 65,000 Target items in as soon as an hour by shopping approximately 1,500 stores in forty-eight states.

Target CEO Brian Cornell graduated from UCLA, has loved UCLA basketball since he was a kid, and embraced many of the philosophies of legendary UCLA basketball coach John Wooden, who once said, "It's what you learn after you know it all that counts."

Target is what it is today because it went the extra mile under Cornell's leadership to be something more than what it had been in the past. Target—and the companies that led up to the forming of Target—failed at times, but always found ways to learn more and overcome those failures and find success. Here are some of the lessons to be learned from Target's story:

Quality management matters. Ever since Target's origin in 1902 as Dayton Dry Goods Company, quality management led the company.

Founder George Draper Dayton maintained a lofty set of personal ethics that he brought to the department store. Those values were adhered to in the years that followed when the baton was passed to his sons and grandsons.

Once Dayton's fell totally into their control, the family members could have chosen to live their lives as wealthy citizens of Minneapolis. Instead, they elected to expand and executed their due diligence in doing so. As the department store grew outside of Minneapolis, the Dayton family's prudence led to other opportunities—like the birth of Target, a discount store of quality reminiscent of the basement store that began in Dayton's.

The Dayton family members in management made the right moves by going public and setting in place guidelines for corporate governance once the Dayton family no longer was represented in the company's leadership.

That would pave the way for quality leaders to emerge, most notably Bob Ulrich—who helped take Target to unprecedented heights—and current CEO and chairman Brian Cornell, whose insights led the chain out of despair and into its current position in the world of retail.

Customers and community always come first. George Dayton ran Dayton's using said ideology. He also believed in supporting his community. Under the founder's philosophy, Dayton's established an unprecedented level of giving back to the community, which his sons and grandsons continued. In addition to the charity, the company brought jobs, and spent money in the community. The citizens of Minneapolis—and even Minnesota—felt as though they were partners with Dayton's, and later Target.

That relationship paid off in the 1990s when the Dayton Corporation got targeted by a corporate raider. They sought help from the people of Minnesota, and received it in the form of a legislature that managed to stave off the hostile takeover.

Target's philosophy also kept the customers and their community in mind: "Expect more. Pay less." That feeling has always helped Target attract customers to the store, and it continues to do so—even after it seemed as though brick-and-mortar retail had died.

Concentrate on what you're good at. Too many irons in the fire can lead to a loss of direction. Target learned that lesson the hard way when it chose to enter Canada on a large scale rather than by proceeding incrementally, as it had always done in the States, and by operating its own pharmacy.

Target realized the error of its ways and closed its Canadian stores, taking a financial beating in the process. Guiding that decision was the fact that Target was not providing the same Target experience in Canada that it was providing to guests in the United States. By shutting down the Canadian stores, Target realized that it could sharpen its efforts in the United States, where the company had always excelled.

Despite the revenue streams created by its pharmacy operations, Target opted to sell out those interests to CVS, which in turn operated their stores inside Target stores. While Target forfeited an opportunity to make more money through its own pharmacy operation, the decision to focus on what it was best at—while continuing to offer CVS's pharmaceutical services inside Target stores—proved to be the right tactic.

Identify and remain true to your brand. Target came into being in 1962, the same year that Kmart and Walmart went into business. Kmart and Walmart were discount stores—as was Target, only Target became a discount store with a twist by quickly evolving into the quality discount store.

Being associated with an upscale department store such as Dayton's didn't hurt that perception either. The slogan "Expect more. Pay less." further reminded customers what shopping at Target meant.

Offering unique designer brands, such as those created by Michael Graves, delivered surprises to shoppers—and quality. That chic element that defined the Target brand was reflected in the way that customers referred to the retail chain as "Tar-zhay," as if shopping there was like stepping into a highbrow boutique.

Target lost its mojo for a number of years when it strayed from delivering on the "expect more" aspect of its promise and instead only delivered on "pay less." Target refocused, and has since rectified this perception by returning to its roots. The brand's slogan is alive and well today, and it appears as though staying true to it will allow the company to thrive in the future.

Don't be afraid to take chances. Fortune favors the bold as the old saying goes, and Target personifies it through its actions. From the moment the Dayton brothers decided that they wanted to build something great rather than sit on their fortunes, Target's DNA has possessed an element of courage and valued taking chances. Colossal failures could have followed.

The brothers decided to expand Dayton's. They opted to open the first US indoor mall. They decided to partner with J.L. Hudson's of Detroit. And, ultimately, they went all in to start Target—each of those risks turned into solid decisions.

When Target seemed to have lost its way with its Canadian troubles and in the aftermath of the data breach, Target's board decided to reach outside of the bullseye family to hire an outsider to become CEO and chairman. Brian Cornell's hiring has paid off handsomely ever since, and part of that success can be attributed to the fact that he is not afraid to take chances.

Cornell's decision to go all in with brick-and-mortar retail, at a time when most experts thought such a decision to be absurd, might be the best decision the company has made in its storied history.

Opportunities

Target is constantly looking to bolster talent throughout the company. One of Target's goals is to make sure they have the team that can deliver for its guests. So they take care of that team and they create an environment where they don't dread going to work.[1]

Target employs over 350,000 people[2] across a variety of positions in its stores, distribution centers, tech centers, and corporate offices. Known for celebrating diversity and employees who represent their surrounding communities, Target appreciates candidates of different backgrounds, experiences, and points of view. They are constantly seeking applicants with strong ties to their community, who have volunteer experience and positive attitudes.

Plenty of opportunities exist within Target's 1,868 stores spread over fifty states and the District of Columbia. Other jobs are available in the company's forty-one distribution centers,[3] the corporate headquarters in Minneapolis, the five additional offices[4] across the United States, the global capabilities center in Bangalore, India, and over a dozen sourcing offices globally.

Corporate careers at Target include:[5] administrative support; assets protection and corporate security; business operations; call centers & financial retail services; finance & accounting;

food & beverage; global supply chain & logistics; human resources; legal affairs, risk & compliance; marketing, media, & communications; merchandising & global sourcing; product design & development; project management; real estate design & property management; strategy & innovation; and technology & data sciences.

Store leadership roles include: team leader; store director; executive team leader; and district senior director.

Store hourly roles include: specialty sales; service & engagement; general merchandise & food sales; and support roles.

Distribution center leadership roles include: distribution center leadership; transportation and logistics; engineering and facilities; and supply chain, logistics, & fulfillment.

Distribution center hourly roles include: warehouse operations; packing operations; logistics/transportation; food distribution; engineering & facilities; administrative/clerical; assets protection; and human resources.

Kremer said the great American dream remains alive at Target, where employees, metaphorically, can still advance from the mail room to the corporate office.

"One in four of our store directors is promoted internally, so comes up through the ranks," Kremer said. "We also are supplementing that with an external recruitment strategy, so that you have a blend of both. Historically, Target hired straight out of campus and we grew the talent. That's still very much a strategy that we pride ourselves on. But five or six years ago, we recognized you also need some external perspective. So very intentionally infusing talent from outside the company into these spaces that were newer to us became a really important part of the overall talent strategy."[6]

Kremer noted that Target has many entry-level leadership development programs in its stores and headquarters.

Should I Work There?

Given the many different positions at Target across multiple tiers of labor, finding a soup-to-nuts answer is difficult. Reviews about working at Target on various job boards vary from Target being the best place anyone could work to the dregs of the universe. Given the subjective nature of said reviews, it would be difficult to get the definitive answer for whether one should seek employment at Target. Perhaps the age-old supply-and-demand formula is the best way to answer the question: people want to work at Target.

Kremer allowed that in 2013 and 2014, "it was more difficult to recruit talent to Target" when the company's strategy was less clear and the culture "had some cracks in it. Fast-forward to today, and we have people knocking on the door [to work at Target]," Kremer said. "People see the business performance. They see that there are great big fun problems to solve in retail. So it's a different recruiting story than it was six years ago.

"Couple that with our focus. If I think about our hourly population, we made a game-changing investment in wage [full-circle hourly wage improvements were scheduled to be in effect by the end of 2020]. Couple that with our family-focused benefits. . . . Our philosophy is to offer those benefits to all who work for Target—different than maybe some of our competitors that are more focused on their full-time population. We are focused on part-time and full-time population. So it's not only the wage but the focus on really family-friendly benefits combined with that culture. That's the way we got to market."[7]

Employees can still advance through the ranks, and Target offers them the means to make those progressions. For example, Human Resources has a learning-and-development team that focuses on in-role training to ensure that employees have the necessary skills to do their job.

"That team also focusses on supporting team members with learning and development for next roles," Kremer said. "That is part of what we offer to the team member base. We also invest heavy in leadership development."[8]

Investment in development goes all the way to the top tier of Target's executives. Kremer cited a "major investment" in a weeklong developmental program for leaders from the vice-president level on up. The program focused on change management, setting vision, strategy, and the cross-function ways of working.

"That's been absolutely a highlight for our officer team," Kremer said. "Driving engagement and retention in really positive ways with our officer team. So it's a multi-pronged approach to learning and development. Train in role, train for next role, and train leaders."[9]

Brian Cornell cited Target's long history of recruiting college interns. "We have a big MBA class; we bring hundreds of interns in every summer," Cornell said. "And largely from Big Ten schools, a few from Notre Dame. And, this company has always had a big commitment to talent development. So, for many of the leaders who are in the building today, they joined us after being an intern. Five years later, they were in management positions. Twenty years later, they're officers. And thirty years later, they retire. So we've always had this great commitment to talent development."[10]

Many job opportunities exist at Target, and there are avenues for advancement—even from the lowest ranks. If you find a job at Target, the opportunity will come down to what you make of it.

ACKNOWLEDGMENTS

Many thanks to Target for their help in gathering information for this book, most notably Brian Cornell, Rick Gomez, John Mulligan, and Melissa Kremer. In addition, I'd like to thank those who provided background information during my on-site visits to Target stores and the corporate office. Also, I salute Amanda Cowden, Robert Wood, Sean Madigan, Jacqueline DeBuse, Amy Koch, and Erin Conroy for their efforts with the manuscript. Special thanks to Drew Halunen, who facilitated my visit to Minneapolis and answered many questions.

Finally, thanks to Kevin Anderson & Associates.

ENDNOTES

Chapter 1

1. Brian Cornell, 2018 Target Corporate Responsibility Report, 3.
2. Brian Cornell, interview by author, October 7, 2019.
3. Bruce B. Dayton and Ellen B. Green, *George Draper Dayton: A Man of Parts* (privately published biography, 1997), 29.
4. Bruce B. Dayton and Ellen B. Green, *George Draper Dayton: A Man of Parts*, 32.
5. Bruce B. Dayton and Ellen B. Green, *George Draper Dayton: A Man of Parts*, 32.
6. "Mrs. G. D. Dayton Dies Following Week's Illness," *Minneapolis Tribune,* January 20, 1931.
7. Stephen George, *Enterprising Minnesotans, 150 Years of Business Pioneers* (Minnesota: University of Minnesota Press, 2005), 77.
8. "Geo. D. Dayton Funeral Will Be on Monday," *Minneapolis Star Tribune,* February 19, 1938.
9. Bruce B. Dayton and Ellen B. Green, *George Draper Dayton: A Man of Parts*, 195.
10. "George D. Dayton Dies at 80," *Minneapolis Star,* February 18, 1938.
11. Richard Heath, "Historic Minneapolis Fires—1895," *Extra Alarmer,* September 26, 1895.
12. Richard Heath, "Historic Minneapolis Fires—1895."
13. "Church in Flames," *St. Paul Globe,* September 6, 1895.
14. Reference for Business, referenceforbusiness.com/history/2/19/Target-Corporation.html.
15. "Westminster Site Sold," *Saint Paul Globe,* April 7, 1896.
16. "Westminster Site Sold," *Saint Paul Globe,* April 7, 1896.

17. Iric Nathanson, "The Dayton Name: A Minnesota Institution Since 1903," *MINNPOST*, December 10, 2010.

18. "Strong Protest Sent in by the City Engineer," *Saint Paul Globe*, June 25, 1989.

19. "Balked by 'Limits,'" *Minneapolis Journal*, February 16, 1901.

20. "Another Handsome Nicollet Avenue Block," *Minneapolis Journal*, March 16, 1901.

21. "Dayton Sees Need of More Loop Building," *Minneapolis Star*, January 19, 1929.

22. Bruce B. Dayton and Ellen B. Green, *George Draper Dayton: A Man of Parts*, 241.

23. "The Daylight Store," *Minneapolis Journal*, June 25, 1902.

24. Stephen George, *Enterprising Minnesotans, 150 Years of Business Pioneers*, 78.

25. "Dayton's: More Than a Century of Minnesota Retail," *MINNPOST*, September 29, 2015.

26. "Snapshots Taken at Deauville, France, by Theodore Mayer, of the Dayton Company," *Minneapolis Morning Tribune*, September 23, 1913.

27. "History Has Been Written in the Past Few Days," *Minneapolis Morning Tribune*, May 14, 1920.

28. Dayton's Advertisement, *Minneapolis Morning Tribune*, September 22, 1920.

29. Paul Nelson, "Dayton's: More Than a century of Minnesota Retail," *MINNPOST*, September 29, 2015.

30. "Amateur Modistes Display Creations," *Minneapolis Morning Tribune*, October 23, 1920.

31. "Little Mothers and Dolls Attend a Tea d'enfant," *Minneapolis Sunday Tribune*, November 2, 1913.

32. Dayton's Advertisement, *Minneapolis Morning Tribune*, October 13, 1922.

33. History of Dayton Hudson Corporation, *Reference for Business*.

34. "1,700 Dayton Employees, Friends Picnic Guests," *Minneapolis Sunday Tribune*, July 18, 1920.

35. Dayton's Advertisement, *Minneapolis Morning Tribune*, December 7, 1917.

36. Bruce B. Dayton and Ellen B. Green, *George Draper Dayton: A Man of Parts*, 355.

37. Robert Grimm, ed., *Notable American Philanthropists, Biographies of Giving and Volunteering*, 76–77.
38. "George D. Dayton Dies at 80," *Minneapolis Star*, February 18, 1938.
39. "George D. Dayton Dies at 80," *Minneapolis Star*, February 18, 1938.

Chapter 2

1.   "Goodfellow's New Store Is Ideal," *Minneapolis Tribune*, June 25, 1902.
2.   "Draper Dayton, Prominent Merchant of Minneapolis, Dies at Minnetonka Home," *Minnesota Daily Star*, July 26, 1923.
3.   "Draper Dayton, Prominent Merchant of Minneapolis, Dies at Minnetonka Home," *Minnesota Daily Star*, July 26, 1923.
4.   Bruce B. Dayton and Ellen B. Green, *George Draper Dayton: A Man of Parts*, 246
5.   "G. N. Dayton, Store Head, Dies at 63," *Minneapolis Morning Tribune*, April 1, 1950.
6.   "G. N. Dayton, Store Head, Dies at 63," *Minneapolis Morning Tribune*, April 1, 1950.
7.   Robert Grimm, ed., *Notable American Philanthropists, Biographies of Giving and Volunteering*, 76.
8.   Robert Grimm, ed., *Notable American Philanthropists, Biographies of Giving and Volunteering*, 76–77.
9.   Laura Rowley, *On Target, How the World's Hottest Retailer Hit a Bull's-Eye* (Hoboken, NJ: Wiley, 2003), 104.
10. "G. N. Dayton, Store Head, Dies at 63," *Minneapolis Morning Tribune*, April 1, 1950.

Chapter 3

1.   *Minneapolis Star Tribune*, June 23, 1989.
2.   Bruce B. Dayton and Ellen B. Green, *The Birth of Target* (Minnesota: privately published, 2008), 22.
3.   Bruce B. Dayton and Ellen B. Green, *The Birth of Target*, 22.
4.   Wayne Christensen, "The Decade of the Daytons: The Downtown Dynasty Has Influence Far Beyond the Department Store Walls," *Corporate Report*, January 1979, 38.
5.   Bruce B. Dayton and Ellen B. Green, *The Birth of Target*, 23.

6. Claire Suddath, "A Brief History of the Middle Class," *TIME*, February 27, 2009.

7. Bruce B. Dayton and Ellen B. Green, *The Birth of Target*, 25.

8. Wayne Christensen, "The Decade of the Daytons," 38.

9. "Dayton's Will Sell Store in Sioux Falls," *Minneapolis Star*, March 17, 1967.

10. Malcolm Gladwell, "The Terrazzo Jungle," *New Yorker*, March 15, 2004.

11. Malcolm Gladwell, "The Terrazzo Jungle."

12. Bruce B. Dayton and Ellen B. Green, *The Birth of Target*, 30.

13. Malcolm Gladwell, "The Terrazzo Jungle."

14. Paul Lukas, "Our Malls, Ourselves," *Fortune*, October 18, 2004.

15. Paul Lukas, "Our Malls, Ourselves."

16. Paul Lukas, "Our Malls, Ourselves."

17. John Wickland, "$20,000,000 Southdale Center Opens Monday," *Minneapolis Sunday Tribune*, October 7, 1956.

18. Neal St. Anthony, David Phelps, and Mary Abbe, "We Just Lost a Minnesota Giant," *Star Tribune*, November 14, 2015.

19. "Southdale Is a Dream Come True for Third-General Daytons," *Minneapolis Sunday Tribune*, October 7, 1956.

20. Ken Roberts, *Minnesota 150: The People, Places and Things That Shape Our State* (Minnesota Historical Society Press, October 15, 2007), 159.

21. "Southdale Is a Dream Come True for Third-General Daytons," *Star Tribune*, October 7, 1956.

22. Bruce B. Dayton and Ellen B. Green, *The Birth of Target*, 46.

23. "Wells Joins Dayton Co. Directors," *Minneapolis Star*, December 11, 1963.

24. "Stuart Wells, Dayton Store Head Dies," *Minneapolis Tribune*, December 18, 1967.

25. Hadlai A. Hull Obit, *Star Tribune*, August 14, 2011.

26. Hadlai A. Hull Obit, *Star Tribune*, August 14, 2011.

27. "Curry Is Elected Vice-President of Dayton Corp.," *Minneapolis Tribune*, December 14, 1967.

28. Bruce B. Dayton and Ellen B. Green, *The Birth of Target*, 48.

29. Bruce B. Dayton and Ellen B. Green, *The Birth of Target*, 49.

30. Bruce B. Dayton and Ellen B. Green, *The Birth of Target*, 54.

31. Bruce B. Dayton and Ellen B. Green, *The Birth of Target*, 52.

Chapter 4

1. "Retailing: Everybody Loves a Bargain," *TIME*, July 6, 1962.
2. "Retailing: Everybody Loves a Bargain," *TIME*, July 6, 1962.
3. "Simple Formula for Success," *Courier-Post*, August 30, 1961.
4. David Halberstam, *The Fifties*, 151.
5. "Retailing: Everybody Loves a Bargain," *TIME*, July 6, 1962.
6. Marc Levinson, Interview with *Morning Edition*, NPR, November 19, 2012.
7. Bruce B. Dayton and Ellen B. Green, *The Birth of Target*, 56.
8. Bruce B. Dayton and Ellen B. Green, *The Birth of Target*, 56.
9. Dayton's Advertisement, *Minneapolis Star*, September 10, 1959.
10. "John Geisse, 71, Dies; Helped Start Target, Wholesale Stores," *Star Tribune*, February 23, 1992.
11. "John F. Geisse, 71; Founded Venture Discount Stores Here," *St. Louis Post-Dispatch*, February 23, 1992.
12. Curt Matthews, "Experience for May Company," *St. Louis Post-Dispatch*, January 28, 1970.
13. "May Co to Enter Discount Department Store Business," *Valley News*, September 1, 1968.
14. Arthur Markowitz, "From Roseville to Greatland, Target Still Hits the Mark," *Discount Store News*, September 17, 1990.
15. Curt Matthews, "Experience for May Company," *St. Louis Post-Dispatch*, January 28, 1970.
16. "John F. Geisse, 71; Founded Venture Discount Stores Here," *St. Louis Post-Dispatch*, February 23, 1992.
17. Curt Matthews, "Experience for May Company."
18. Bob Ylvisaker, "Daytons Plan Discount Store Chain," *Star Tribune* July 9, 1961.
19. Arthur Markowitz, "From Roseville to Greatland, Target Still Hits the Mark."
20. Arthur Markowitz, "From Roseville to Greatland, Target Still Hits the Mark."
21. Bob Ylvisaker, "Daytons Plan Discount Store Chain."
22. Bob Ylvisaker, "Daytons Plan Discount Store Chain."

Chapter 5

1. Mae Anderson, "Company Logos Can Help Make an Impact," Associated Press, July 22, 2012.
2. "Dayton Sees Buyer Benefit in Retailing Revolution," *Minneapolis Morning Tribune*, February 17, 1962.
3. Bruce B. Dayton and Ellen B. Green, *The Birth of Target*, 63.
4. "J. F. Geiss, Who Founded Discount Stores," *New York Times*, February 27, 1992.
5. Laura Rowley, *On Target, How the World's Hottest Retailer Hit a Bull's-Eye*, 117.
6. "Target after 50 Years: Retailer Transformed How America Shops," *Pioneer Press*, May 12, 2012.
7. "Target to Open Second Suburban Discount Store Thursday in Crystal," *Minneapolis Sunday Tribune*, September 2, 1962.
8. Bruce B. Dayton and Ellen B. Green, *The Birth of Target*, 60.
9. Bruce B. Dayton and Ellen B. Green, *The Birth of Target*, 60.
10. Bruce B. Dayton and Ellen B. Green, *The Birth of Target*, 63.
11. Laura Rowley, *On Target, How the World's Hottest Retailer Hit a Bull's-Eye*, 127.
12. Harvey D. Shapiro, "The Daytons of Dayton Hudson: The Family Merchants of Dayton Hudson at a Glance," *New York Times*, June 17, 1979.
13. Bruce B. Dayton and Ellen B. Green, *The Birth of Target*, 88.
14. Bruce B. Dayton and Ellen B. Green, *The Birth of Target*, 89.
15. "Four 'Outside' Directors Elected by Dayton Corp.," *Star Tribune*, September 7, 1967.
16. Hallock Seymour, "Dayton Shares Put on Market," *Minneapolis Star*, October 18, 1967.
17. Arthur Markowitz, "From Roseville to Greatland, Target Still Hits the Mark."
18. Bruce B. Dayton and Ellen B. Green, *The Birth of Target*, 96.

Chapter 6

1. Clay Latimer, "Harry Cunningham Led a Retail Revolution at Kmart," *Investor's Business Daily*, March 25, 2013.
2. Kmart Company History.

3. Clay Latimer, "Harry Cunningham Led a Retail Revolution at Kmart."

4. Sam Walton, *Sam Walton, Made in America: My Story* (New York: Doubleday, 1992), 5, 15, 20.

5. Alex Planes, "How Walmart Became the World's Biggest Retailer: Learning from the Market's Past to Understand Its Present," *Motley Fool*, July 2, 2013.

6. Walmart Corporate History, https://corporate.walmart.com /our-story/our-history.

7. Sam Walton, *Sam Walton, Made in America: My Story*, 46.

8. Thomas C. Hayes, "Sam Walton Is Dead at 74; the Founder of Walmart Stores: Sam Walton, Walmart Founder, Dies," *New York Times*, April 6, 1992.

9. Alex Planes, "How Walmart Became the World's Biggest Retailer."

10. Alex Planes, "How Walmart Became the World's Biggest Retailer."

11. "Discount Store Plan by May Co.," *St. Louis Post-Dispatch*, August 30, 1968.

12. Laura Rowley, *On Target, How the World's Hottest Retailer Hit a Bull's-Eye*, 129.

13. Curt Matthews, "Experience for May Company."

14. Curt Matthews, "Experience for May Company."

15. Curt Matthews, "Experience for May Company."

16. Curt Matthews, "Experience for May Company."

17. Marianne Taylor, "Walmart Acquiring Club Rival," *Chicago Tribune*, November 7, 1990.

18. Dick Youngblood, "Dayton Hudson Full Speed Ahead," *Star Tribune*, April 11, 1976.

Chapter 7

1. Dick Youngblood, "Dayton Hudson Full Speed Ahead."

2. Dick Youngblood, "Dayton Hudson Full Speed Ahead."

3. Hank Greenberg, "One-Time Salesman Turns Target Stores Around," *Des Moines Tribune*, September 15, 1977.

4. Dick Youngblood, "Dayton Hudson Full Speed Ahead."

5. Dick Youngblood, "Dayton Hudson Full Speed Ahead."

6. Hank Greenberg, "One-Time Salesman Turns Target Stores Around."

7. Hank Greenberg, "One-Time Salesman Turns Target Stores Around."

8. David Mehegan, "Tales of a Retail Doctor," *Boston Globe*, June 19, 1990.

9. Janet Key, "Montgomery Ward Swimming against Current of Red Ink," *Chicago Tribune*, October 14, 1981.

10. Hank Greenberg, "One-Time Salesman Turns Target Stores Around."

11. Janet Key, "Montgomery Ward Swimming against Current of Red Ink."

12. David Mehegan, "Tales of a Retail Doctor," *Boston Globe*, June 19, 1990.

13. Pamela Klein, "New Ames Chief a Cocky $8 Million Man," *Hartford Courant* (ran in the *Indianapolis Star*), May 20, 1990.

14. Pamela Klein, "New Ames Chief a Cocky $8 Million Man."

15. Hank Greenberg, "One-Time Salesman Turns Target Stores Around."

16. Hank Greenberg, "One-Time Salesman Turns Target Stores Around."

17. Hank Greenberg, "One-Time Salesman Turns Target Stores Around."

18. Hank Greenberg, "One-Time Salesman Turns Target Stores Around."

19. Hank Greenberg, "One-Time Salesman Turns Target Stores Around."

20. Hank Greenberg, "One-Time Salesman Turns Target Stores Around."

21. Hank Greenberg, "One-Time Salesman Turns Target Stores Around."

22. Hank Greenberg, "One-Time Salesman Turns Target Stores Around."

23. Hank Greenberg, "One-Time Salesman Turns Target Stores Around."

24. Dale Kasler, "Iowa Native Macke Takes the Field," *Des Moines Register*, May 27, 1990.

25. Dale Kasler, "Iowa Native Macke Takes the Field."

26. Arthur Markowitz, "From Roseville to Greatland, Target Still Hits the Mark."

27. Susan Chandler, "Designers Finding Their Target," *Chicago Tribune*, August 19, 2001.
28. Arthur Markowitz, "From Roseville to Greatland, Target Still Hits the Mark."
29. Willard N. Ander and Neil Z. Stern, *Winning at Retail: Developing a Sustained Model for Retail Success* (John Wiley & Sons, 2007).
30. From "Guides for Growth" provided by Target.
31. From "Guides for Growth" provided by Target.
32. Laura Rowley, *On Target, How the World's Hottest Retailer Hit a Bull's-Eye*, 144.
33. From "Guides for Growth" provided by Target.
34. "Target Celebrates Half-Century of Retailing Excellence," *MMR* (Vol. 29, issue 8), May 14, 2012.
35. "Dayton-Hudson's Hard Push for National Clout," *Business Week*, September 8, 1980.
36. From "Guides for Growth" provided by Target.
37. Frank Allen, "Shelves in Target Soon to Be Bare of *Playboy*," *Minneapolis Star*, May 17, 1977.
38. Frank Allen, "Shelves in Target Soon to Be Bare of *Playboy*."
39. Frank Allen, "Shelves in Target Soon to Be Bare of *Playboy*."
40. Hank Greenberg, "One-Time Salesman Turns Target Stores Around."
41. Dick Youngblood, "Dayton Hudson Full Speed Ahead."
42. David Schulz, "The Nation's Retail Power Players/2006," *WaybackMachine*, July 12, 2006.
43. On Target Newsletter, November 1981, 4.
44. Cathy Mong, "Ayr-Way Stores to Be Right on Target," *Palladium-Item*, November 5, 1980.
45. "Target Expands Westward," *Minneapolis Star*, January 20, 1982.
46. Susan Feyder, "Target to Open 33 Stores in Western States," *Minneapolis Star and Tribune*, August 6, 1982.
47. Susan Feyder, "Target to Open 33 Stores in Western States."
48. Neal St. Anthony, "Dayton's Fashioning a Comeback," *Minneapolis Star and Tribune*, May 25, 1987.
49. Dan Wascoe Jr., "Target Opens 30 New Stores in Dixie," *Star Tribune*, May 1, 1989.

Chapter 8

1. Bruce B. Dayton and Ellen B. Green, *The Birth of Target*, 101.
2. Bruce B. Dayton and Ellen B. Green, *The Birth of Target*, 101.
3. "Civic Leader, Arts Philanthropist Ken Dayton Dies at 80," *Star Tribune*, July 21, 2003.
4. Kenneth N. Dayton, "Corporate Governance: The Other Side of the Coin," *Harvard Business Review*, January 1984.
5. Bruce B. Dayton and Ellen B. Green, *The Birth of Target*, 102.
6. Bruce B. Dayton and Ellen B. Green, *The Birth of Target*, 104.
7. Bruce B. Dayton and Ellen B. Green, *The Birth of Target*, 54.
8. Bruce B. Dayton and Ellen B. Green, *The Birth of Target*, 124.
9. Marisa Helms and Dan Olson, "Remembering Kenneth Dayton," Minnesota Public Radio, July 21, 2003.
10. Bruce B. Dayton and Ellen B. Green, *The Birth of Target*, 125.
11. Maura Lerner, "Hafts Approach Second Offering as Suitors Instead of Raiders," *Star Tribune*, September 18, 1987.
12. Josephine Marcotty, "Dart made tens of millions in previous takeover battles," *Minneapolis Star and Tribune*, June 20, 1987.
13. Caroline E. Mayer, "One Year After the Haft's Bid, Safeway is Leaner, More Efficient," *Washington Post*, August 30, 1987.
14. Josephine Marcotty, "New State Law Won't Apply Unless Hafts Offer Turns Hostile," *Star Tribune*, September 18, 1987.

Chapter 9

1. "Target Plans 35 Northwest Stores, Expansion of California Distribution," *Minneapolis Star and Tribune*, March 19, 1987.
2. Dan Wascoe Jr., "Target Opens 30 new stores in Dixie."
3. Dan Wascoe Jr., "Target Opens 30 new stores in Dixie."
4. Dale Kasler, "Dayton Says Plans Stay on Target," *Des Moines Register*, May 27, 1990.
5. Dan Wascoe Jr., "Days of Double Coupons Are Increasingly Numbered," *Star Tribune*, September 17, 1990.
6. Dan Wascoe Jr., "Target's New Apple Valley Store Is Indeed Great, as in 'Large,'" *Minneapolis Star Tribune*, September 29, 1990.
7. Susan Feyder, "New Dayton Hudson CEO Seen as Aggressive, Creative," *Star Tribune*, April 15, 1994.

8. Jackie Crosby, "A Working Life Spent On-Target," *Minneapolis Star Tribune*, April 27, 2008.

9. Jackie Crosby, "A Working Life Spent On-Target."

10. "Wal-Mart's Ads Misleading, Target Says," *St. Cloud Times*, March 25, 1993.

11. Dick Youngblood, "Frustration Might Have Played a Part in Ken Macke's Departure," *Minneapolis Star Tribune*, April 15, 1994.

12. Sally Apgar, "Dayton Hudson Crossroads," *Star Tribune*, July 23, 1995.

13. Jackie Crosby, "A Working Life Spent On-Target."

14. Sally Apgar, "Without Boundaries: Dayton Hudson Touts Philosophies That Are Reshaping the Corporation," *Star Tribune*, March 12, 1996.

15. Jackie Crosby, "A Working Life Spent On-Target."

16. Sally Apgar, "The Man from Target to Usher in New Era, But How Is the Question," *Star Tribune*, June 21, 1994.

17. Sally Apgar, "The Man from Target to Usher in New Era, But How Is the Question."

18. Sally Apgar, "The Man from Target to Usher in New Era, But How Is the Question."

19. Melissa Levy, "Target Shareholders Left with Questions," *Star Tribune*, May 22, 2003.

20. Laura Rowley, *On Target, How the World's Hottest Retailer Hit a Bull's-Eye*, 79.

21. Janet Moore, "Dayton Hudson CEO Calls for More Improvements," *Star Tribune*, May 22, 1997.

22. Glen Creno, "Department-Store Chain Recharges Its Image," *Arizona Republic*, June 12, 1997.

23. Jackie Crosby, "A Working Life Spent On-Target."

24. Neal St. Anthony, "Santabear Looks for a Place Beside Rudolph, Frosty," *Star Tribune*, November 16, 1986.

25. Dan Wascoe, Jr., "His Marketing Visions Bear Well for Dayton's," Star Tribune, May 25, 1987.

26. Dan Wascoe, Jr., "His Marketing Visions Bear Well for Dayton's."

27. Dan Wascoe, Jr., "His Marketing Visions Bear Well for Dayton's."

28. Dan Wascoe, Jr., "His Marketing Visions Bear Well for Dayton's."

29. Don Wascoe, Jr.," Chain Expands Reach from Coast to Coast, Tests Pricing Strategy," *Star Tribune*, May 1, 1989.

30. Kevin Duchschere, "Target Hits Bull's Eye in Wolves' New Arena," *Star Tribune*, August 8, 1990.

31. Kevin Duchschere, "Target Hits Bull's Eye in Wolves' New Arena."

32. Christmas Doorbusters Almanac, *Target Corp. Archives.*

33. Marla Matzer, "Target's Great White Hope," *Los Angeles Times,* November 27, 1997.

34. Christmas Doorsbusters Almanac, *Target Corp. Archives.*

35. Marla Matzer, "Target's Great White Hope."

36. Target Advertisement, *Star Tribune,* February 20, 1994.

37. Gina Moore, "Club Wedd Takes Brides and Grooms on an Aisle Cruise," *Jackson Sun,* February 16, 1994.

38. Daniela Sternitzky-Di Napoli, "Millennials Are Asking for an Unconventional Wedding Gift," *Houston Chronicle,* June 22, 2016.

39. Kavita Kumar, "Target Will End School Charity Program, Shift Giving Focus to Wellness," *Star Tribune,* September 15, 2015.

40. Tom Ryan, "Target's Mascot Makes a Comeback," *Retail Wire,* December 28, 2015.

41. Susan Krashinsky, "The Secret Life of Target's Mascot, Bullseye," *The Globe and Mail,* March 27, 2013.

42. Alice Z. Cuneo, "ON TARGET; Retailing stardom: Spritely Marketing Makes It Chic to Buy Cheap," *Advertising Age,* December 11, 2000.

43. "Target Completes Marshall Field's Sale to May," *St. Cloud Times,* July 31, 2004.

44. Jackie Crosby, "A Working Life Spent On-Target."

Chapter 10

1. Connie Nelson, "Good Design Comes Home," *Star Tribune,* March 4, 1999.

2. Christopher Hawthorne, "Michael Graves Dies at 80; Pioneering Figure in Postmodern Architecture," *Los Angeles Times,* March 12, 2015.

3. Connie Nelson, "Good Design Comes Home."

4. Connie Nelson, "Good Design Comes Home."

5. Connie Nelson, "Good Design Comes Home."

6. Rosemary Feitelberg, "Designtarget Product ER Talks Shop," *Women's Wear Daily,* March 21, 2006.

7. Rosemary Feitelberg, "Designtarget Product ER Talks Shop."

8. Linda Hales, "Michael Graves Hits the Bull's-Eye with Whimsical Housewares," *Washington Post,* February 26, 1999.

9. Alan Pittman, "Mossimo Takes Aim at the Masses with Target," *Golf World*, April 14, 2000.

10. Vanessa L. Facenda, "Michael v. Martha: More Than Michael," *Retail Merchandizer*, August 2001, 30.

11. Jim McCartney, "Target Pushes 'Cool' Image, Low Prices," *Knight Ridder*, October 17, 1999.

12. Jim McCartney, "Target Pushes 'Cool' Image, Low Prices."

13. Target's Corporate Timeline, CorporateTarget.com.

Chapter 11

1. "Rumor of Target Buyout Boosts Shares of Canada's Hudson Bay," Associated Press, August 14, 2004.

2. Kavita Kumar, "Target's Canadian Rescue Aims at Prices and Supply," *Star Tribune*, August 14, 2014.

3. David Gewitz, "Billion-Dollar Mistake: How Inferior IT Killed Target Canada," ZDNet, February 11, 2016.

4. Joe Castaldo, "THE LAST DAYS OF TARGET, The Untold Tale of Target Canada's Difficult Birth, Tough Life and Brutal Death," *Canadian Business*.

5. Hollie Shaw, "Target Canada Alive and Kicking," *Windsor Star*, May 13, 2014.

6. Joe Castaldo, "THE LAST DAYS OF TARGET."

7. David Gewitz, "Billion-Dollar Mistake: How Inferior IT Killed Target Canada."

8. Joe Castaldo, "THE LAST DAYS OF TARGET."

9. Phil Wahba, "Why Target Failed in Canada," *Fortune*, January 15, 2015.

10. Thomas Lee, "Target Profits Catch the Chills from Canada," *Star Tribune*, August 22, 2013.

11. Mike Hughlett, "Target's Move to the North Went South in Many Ways," *Star Tribune*, January 16, 2015.

12. Hollie Shaw, "Target Canada Alive and Kicking."

13. Mike Hughlett, "Target's Move to the North Went South in Many Ways."

14. Krystina Gustafson, "Target Apologizes to 'Disappointed' Canada Shoppers," CNBC, June 17, 2014.

15. "The Target Data Breach One Year Later," Minnesota Public Radio, December 8, 2014.

16. Alexandrea Roman, "How to Not Get Fired: Lessons from Target CEO Gregg Steinhafel's Exit," *Convene*, September 23, 2019.
17. "Statement from Target's Board of Directors," *A Bullseye View* (Target's company blog), May 5, 2014.
18. David Gill, "Target Turnover," *HFN Home Furnishings News*, June 1, 2014.

Chapter 12

1. Melissa Kremer, interview by author, October 8, 2019.
2. Target company release, July 31, 2014.
3. "A New Era at Target," *MMR*, August 18, 2014.
4. John Mulligan, interview by author, October 7, 2019.
5. Brian Cornell, interview by author, October 7, 2019.
6. "Cornell asked to 'Move Target Forward,'" *Chain Drug Review*, August 11, 2014.
7. "CEO is Bullish on Transformation Plan," *MMR*, March 23, 2015.
8. Phil Wahba, "Target Has a New CEO: Will He Re-energize the Retailer?" *Fortune*, February 19, 2015.
9. Jackie Crosby, "A Boss on 'Target,'" *Star Tribune*, August 1, 2014.
10. Walter Loeb, "Target's New CEO Brian Cornell Lacks Innovative Pizzazz," *Forbes*, August 1, 2014.
11. Rick Gomez, interview by author, October 7, 2019.
12. Brian Cornell, interview by author, October 7, 2019.
13. "A New Era at Target," *MMR*, August 18, 2014.
14. Brian Cornell, interview by author, October 7, 2019.

Chapter 13

1. Kavita Kumar, "New Target CEO Aims to Learn, Listen Initially," *Star Tribune*, August 15, 2014.
2. Kavita Kumar, "Target Pep Rally Starts Quest to Be 'Cool Again,'" *Star Tribune*, September 11, 2014.
3. Brian Cornell, interview by author, October 7, 2019.
4. Brian Cornell, interview by author, October 7, 2019.
5. John Mulligan, interview by author, October 7, 2019.
6. Brian Cornell, interview by author, October 7, 2019.

7. Rick Gomes, interview by author, October 7, 2019.

8. Phil Wahba, "Target Has a New CEO: Will He Re-energize the Retailer," *Fortune*, February 19, 2015.

9. "Why Target Lost Its Aim; American Retailing," *Economist*, February 28, 2015.

10. Brian Cornell, "Brian Cornell Addresses Questions about Exiting Canada," *A Bullseye View* (Target Company Blog), January 15, 2015.

11. Brian Cornell, interview by author, October 7, 2019.

12. Brian Cornell, "Brian Cornell Addresses Questions about Exiting Canada."

13. "After Struggle, Target Decides to Exit Canada," *Chain Drug Review*, April 27, 2015.

14. Brian Cornell, "Brian Cornell Addresses Questions about Exiting Canada."

Chapter 14

1. "Cornell Puts His Stamp on Target," *MMR*, May 25, 2015.

2. "Cornell Puts His Stamp on Target."

3. Rick Gomez, interview by author, October 7, 2019.

4. Rick Gomez, interview by author, October 7, 2019.

5. Rick Gomez, interview by author, October 7, 2019.

6. Rick Gomez, interview by author, October 7, 2019.

7. Rick Gomez, interview by author, October 7, 2019.

8. Brian Cornell, interview by author, October 7, 2019.

9. Brian Cornell, interview by author, October 7, 2019.

10. Brian Cornell, interview by author, October 7, 2019.

11. Melissa Kremer, interview by author, October 8, 2019.

12. Melissa Kremer, interview by author, October 8, 2019.

13. John Mulligan, interview with author, October 7, 2019.

14. John Mulligan, interview with author, October 7, 2019.

15. John Mulligan, interview with author, October 7, 2019.

16. John Mulligan, interview with author, October 7, 2019.

17. John Mulligan, interview with author, October 7, 2019.

18. John Mulligan, interview with author, October 7, 2019.

19. John Mulligan, interview with author, October 7, 2019.

20. John Mulligan, interview with author, October 7, 2019.

21. Melissa Kremer, interview by author, October 8, 2019.
22. Sneaha Jha, "How India Is Powering US Retailer Target with Digital Innovations," ETCIO.com. From the *Economic Times*, September 4, 2017.
23. Target company website.

Chapter 15

1. Brian Cornell, interview by author, October 7, 2019.
2. Suzette Parley, "Who Shops Where," *Philadelphia Inquirer*, March 27, 2016.
3. Kavita Kumar, "Target CEO Vows to Reset for Long Term," *Star Tribune*, March 1, 2017.
4. Brian Cornell, interview by author, October 7, 2019.
5. Brian Sozzi, "Target Is the Yahoo Finance 2019 Company of the Year," Yahoo Finance, December 9, 2019.
6. Brian Cornell, interview by author, October 7, 2019.
7. Brian Cornell, interview by author, October 7, 2019.
8. Brian Cornell, interview by author, October 7, 2019.
9. Brian Cornell, interview by author, October 7, 2019.
10. Brian Cornell, interview by author, October 7, 2019.
11. Brian Cornell, interview by author, October 7, 2019.
12. Brian Sozzi, "First Look: Target's 'Store of the Future' Launches in California," The Street, May 19, 2016.
13. Brian Cornell, interview by author, October 7, 2019.
14. Brian Cornell, interview by author, October 7, 2019.
15. Brian Cornell, interview by author, October 7, 2019.
16. Brian Cornell, interview by author, October 7, 2019.
17. Background information provided by Target, October 7, 2019.
18. Observations gathered during visit to mock store, October 7, 2019.
19. Nathanel Meyersohn, "Target's New Strategy Is Paying Off Big Time," CNN Business, August 22, 2018.
20. Brian Sozzi, "Target Is the Yahoo Finance 2019 Company of the Year," Yahoo Finance, December 9, 2019.
21. Brian Cornell, interview by author, October 7, 2019.

Business Lessons and Opportunities

1. Melissa Kremer, interview by author, October 8, 2019.
2. Information from Target website.
3. Information from Target website.
4. Information from Target website.
5. Information from Target website.
6. Melissa Kremer, interview by author, October 8, 2019.
7. Melissa Kremer, interview by author, October 8, 2019.
8. Melissa Kremer, interview by author, October 8, 2019.
9. Melissa Kremer, interview by author, October 8, 2019.
10. Brian Cornell, interview by author, October 7, 2019.

INDEX

HARPERCOLLINS
LEADERSHIP
An Imprint of HarperCollins

THE
SPANX
STORY

Available now from HarperCollins Leadership

CHAPTER ONE

A BILLION-DOLLAR IDEA

Sara Blakely never set out to revolutionize and revive a dying industry, create a new category of clothing, or become a billionaire at age forty-one. As she has told it, all she wanted was to make a good impression at a party.

Standing by her closet door, Sara looked down at the invitation in her hand. For the young, single twenty-seven-year-old, still new to the big city, an invitation to a big social event in a swanky rooftop bar would have been a huge deal. Like many other recent transplants to Atlanta, Georgia, in 1998, Sara had moved there for work. A few months after relocating, she would have met and interacted with many of her coworkers in the offices of Danka, a national business machinery company.

Sara spent several days each week outside of Atlanta, visiting small cities and towns like the one where she'd grown up and been offered her first real job out of college. There at the Danka headquarters, in her cozy beach hometown of Clearwater, Florida, she had started selling fax machines door-to-door.

But it didn't take long for her work ethic and sales results to attract the attention of management. A fast learner and skilled salesperson, she was soon called upon to guide and help others in her department. And when it became clear that Sara was also a skilled instructor, Danka offered her a promotion—out of sales and into the training department at the regional office in Georgia. Now she spent her time teaching other salespeople throughout the country how to get a foot in the door, connect with potential customers, and close the deal.

Naturally outgoing and charismatic, Sara normally had no problem making friends. The invitation to this social gathering created a high-stakes opportunity for Sara. And it had to be more energizing than drinking office coffee while discussing sales strategies for office equipment.

Like everyone preparing to meet new people, Sara knew first impressions matter a great deal. Of course, when she walked into the room, it was important to look her best: professional, put-together, appropriate. The clothes she chose needed to meet those criteria. But it was even more crucial to look *confident* and *relaxed*. To appear confident and relaxed, she needed an outfit that would enable her to *feel* confident and relaxed. And, honestly, was that too much to ask?

That Moment in Front of the Closet

Sara has described in dozens of interviews that moment in front of her closet. And, according to her, the answer to that question was a resounding yes—it *was* too much to ask. Over and over, her eyes kept being drawn to a pair of brand-new white pants that would match perfectly with the light summer blouse and strappy sandals that she had in mind for the party.

But the pants, which had looked amazing on the hanger and beautiful in the dressing room mirror, had yet to be worn out of the house. In fact, they'd hung there in the closet for *eight months* with the tags still on. For one thing, she said that seeing the trousers was a reminder that she'd paid too much for them—nearly $100—not to wear them. According to Sara, her attention immediately went to every imperfection, making her feel insecure and unsure of herself. So, every time, she ended up taking them off, hanging them back up, and changing into something else before leaving the house.

Picturing Sara in 1998, at just twenty-seven, she was pretty, slender, and petite. Her long blonde hair, white teeth, and casual vibe made her look like she'd grown up on the beach—which in fact she had. In her hometown of Clearwater Beach, Florida, Sara said she grew up where everyone wore shorts, flip-flops, and swimsuits—for eleven months out of the year. The professional attire that businesswomen wore in Atlanta was much more structured, formal, and *expensive.* "High fashion and design were foreign to me," Sara said of her life before Atlanta.

Everything moved faster in Atlanta, too (aside from the traffic). People walked fast. Serious people in serious clothing strode purposefully to do serious work for serious employers. The men tended to wear dark-colored suits, ties, and shiny dress shoes. Even on Casual Fridays, they all wore a uniform of sorts, of khaki trousers and golf shirts. But the women's attire really stood out. Many of them seemed to put a lot of effort into looking effortlessly fabulous. In downtown Atlanta, "I noticed everyone dressed up," Sara said, "whether they were working in offices or . . . shopping or having lunch with their friends." On the street, she noticed, "All of the women looked so cute, wearing pretty colorful dresses or little capri pants and high heels." She said she wanted to look like she fit in—thus the white pants. And they didn't just look great on the hanger; every time she put them on, they fit her perfectly. They fit the bill for "effortlessly fabulous"—in every way but the one that counted.

The problem with the pants—in a nutshell—was the rear view. Sara believed they looked amazing everywhere *except* on her rear. The issue was that she could not figure out what to wear *under* them. Regular underwear definitely didn't work— the panty lines were lumpy and clearly visible. They drew attention to her backside for all the wrong reasons. She even tried the pants on over a thong a couple times, but she didn't like how they felt. Plus, thong underwear solved *only* the VPL— visible panty line—problem; they didn't help at all with her other issues. "I was terribly frustrated by not having the right undergarment available," she said, "so I could wear those pants with comfort and confidence."

Only a size two at the time, Sara was both tiny and physically fit. Yet she couldn't help noticing what she described as "some cellulite on the back of my thighs that you could see through the pants." The curve-hugging trousers, both white and thin, made every bump and ripple stand out. That was not confidence-building.

With the party only weeks away, she stood paralyzed in front of her closet. For the anticipated warm summer evening, she'd already settled on a beautiful blouse and her favorite pair of high-heeled sandals. As she considered the bottom half of the outfit, her thoughts kept going back to the white pants. A good mix of businesslike and fashionable, they would project self-confidence and style.

The Shapewear Problem

Sara finally made a decision. This time, she was not going to put the trousers back on the hanger and try to find something else. She was going to wear the damn pants. This called for an undergarment expert.

Taking the pants with her, Sara started visiting local department stores. At each store, after weaving her way through racks to the beige back corner, she explained her problem to a lingerie salesperson. She soon learned that the solution was "shapewear," which she'd never even heard of. But the clerk eagerly pulled several items off the shapewear rack, plopped the stack into her arms, and guided her to the dressing room. Willing to try anything, Sara gamely tried them on.

"When I put on the leggings they suggested, they were so thick," she noted. Plus, she said they "provided more control than I actually needed, which made them extremely uncomfortable." Instead of creating a smooth look under the pants, these undergarments actually created more lumps. Wherever the elastic components had been stitched together, the seams showed clearly through the pants. And even the smoothest underpants dug into her skin at the waist and along their bottom edge, creating ugly "dents" with bulges above and below.

"Those leggings weren't solving my issue. If anything, it made things worse," Sara said.

And she knew right away that she could forget about feeling comfortable in any of them. Every item she tried on made her feel like she was wearing running gear that didn't fit right. Like a bad sports bra, the available shapewear tended to smoosh rather than smooth.

Sara left every store empty-handed. Everything she had found was uncomfortable and totally inadequate. Then it suddenly occurred to her: pantyhose might be a great solution. She knew from experience that a good pair of control-tops would certainly smooth and shape her thighs and rear. And because she could wear them as her only undergarments, she'd have no VPLs.

Back at home, she tried on the whole outfit with pantyhose under the pants, and she was right. She felt and looked amazing—until she looked at her feet. With the hosiery seam obvious on her toes and peeking out of the sandals, she looked like somebody's grandma.

Like most working women in the late 1990s, Sara was familiar with the shortcomings of pantyhose. After all, women at the time were expected to wear pantyhose all day, every day. Many employers spelled out the pantyhose requirement in office dress codes. Women in the southern United States dealt with the heat, itchiness, and overall discomfort of pantyhose at least seven months of the year. For Sara, the only loophole she discovered for skipping pantyhose was when she wore trousers. Only then could she wear sandals without a pantyhose seam.

The day of the party inevitably arrived. Out of other ideas by this point, Sara did the only thing she could think of. She cut the feet off her control-top pantyhose, enabling her to wear what was left of them out of sight under the long pants. And it worked! She felt completely confident and comfortable in the pants. "I looked fabulous, I felt great, I had no panty lines, I looked thinner and smoother," she later said. "I remember thinking, 'This should exist for women.'"

She had no way of knowing that she had just come up with an idea that would change the world, one bottom at a time, and in a few years, make her America's youngest female self-made billionaire.

■ LESSON WE CAN LEARN FROM THE SPANX STORY: DON'T OVERLOOK YOUR OPPORTUNITY

What common problem, obstacle, or annoyance in your daily life can lead you to a breakthrough idea? What are you stepping over that you could or should be turning into a stepping-stone for your success? Open your eyes and look for your opportunity.

The future is within reach.

When you start making your goals a top priority, everything falls into place. Learn from the leaders inspiring millions & apply their strategies to your professional journey.

Leadership Essentials Blog

Activate 180 Podcast

Interactive E-courses

Free templates

Sign up for our free book summaries!
Inspire your next head-turning idea.
hcleadershipessentials.com/pages/book-summaries

LEADERSHIP ESSENTIALS
by HarperCollins Leadership

For more business and leadership advice and resources, visit hcleadershipessentials.com.